"With the skill of a virtuoso, Andy Andrews continues his string of successful writing performances in *The Heart Mender*, his latest entertaining masterpiece. The plot, characters, and storyline combine to summon the reader into an unforgettable experience."

—Robert Silvers
Executive Publisher, *The Saturday Evening Post*

"At the Maui Writers Conference, we have had the best in the country, including filmmakers Ron Howard and James L. Brooks, Pulitzer winners Wendy Wasserstein, Dave Barry, Jimmy Breslin, and Carl Bernstein, best-selling authors Elmore Leonard, Mitch Albom, Robin Cook, Tony Hillerman, John Saul, Elizabeth George, Barbara Kingsolver, and others. Andy Andrews is right at the top of the list. He is mesmerizing, funny, captivating, heartwarming, and just plain ol' good. To have one of his books on your shelf brings his hope-inspiring wisdom into your home."

—Shannon Tullius
Cofounder & Director, Maui Writers Conference

"*The Heart Mender* is a sweeping adventure filled with many emotions. The compelling narrative unites the past and present in a fantastic must-read!"

—Bonnie Tiegel
Senior Supervising Producer, *Entertainment Tonight/The Insider*

"The principle woven into this incredible story has changed my life."

—Tim Brando
CBS Sports Host & Commentator

"If life had a 'reset button'—*The Heart Mender* would be it."

—Joseph Farah
Editor and CEO, WorldNetDaily.com

OTHER BOOKS BY ANDY ANDREWS

⁓

The Traveler's Gift

The Young Traveler's Gift

The Lost Choice

Mastering the Seven Decisions

Socks for Christmas

Return to Sawyerton Springs

The Butterfly Effect

The Noticer

The
HEART
MENDER

A STORY OF SECOND CHANCES

A NDY
A NDREWS

THOMAS NELSON
Since 1798

NASHVILLE DALLAS MEXICO CITY RIO DE JANEIRO

And

To the Stimpson family
of Mobile, Alabama.

Published in Nashville, Tennessee, by Thomas Nelson. Thomas Nelson is a registered trademark of Thomas Nelson, Inc.

Previously published as *Island of Saints* (ISBN 978-0-7852-6140-7).

Thomas Nelson, Inc., titles may be purchased in bulk for educational, business, fund-raising, or sales promotional use. For information, please e-mail SpecialMarkets@ThomasNelson.com.

Interior photos: Jared McDaniel, Studio430.com

Library of Congress Cataloging-in-Publication Data

Andrews, Andy, 1959–
  The heart mender : a story of second chances / Andy Andrews.
    p. cm.
  ISBN 978-0-7852-3103-5
  I. Title.
  PS3601.N5525H43 2010
  813'.6—dc22

                                2009052644

Printed in the United States of America

10 11 12 13 14 WC 6 5 4 3

Author's Note

THE BOOK YOU ARE HOLDING IN YOUR HANDS HAS GENERATED more questions than any work I have ever produced. Therefore, in an effort to satisfy what might become an overwhelming curiosity, maybe it is best that I address those questions for you now—before you begin to read!

I am often asked if I have a favorite among the books I have written. Yes, I do. And this is it. *The Heart Mender* is not only what I believe to be my best work, it is the most compelling—bringing all aspects of a mystery, love story, and thriller to the table in order to deliver a life-changing principle.

What is my greatest career disappointment? Again, I would answer, "This manuscript you hold in your hands." Not this title—just the manuscript. You see, the manuscript was previously published under another name—*Island of Saints*—and for the most part barely even saw a bookstore! Through issues of bad timing, little previous success of my own, and zero publicity, the book was quickly forgotten.

The few people who *did* find the book, however, became (and remain) extremely vocal about their love for the story and its power. Soon a movie producer found it, and the ball, which had seemed lost in deep weeds, started rolling again.

Now released with a more appropriate title, the backing

of a happy publishing company, and a few rabid supporters who still call this their favorite book, *The Heart Mender* is ready to go. And now there is only *the biggest question of all* waiting to be answered . . .

"Is this story true?"

Without exception, every person who has read this book has asked that question.

And the answer is . . . yes . . . for the most part. All the numbers, the history, the dates, and the items I found are real. I have changed some locations and most of the names. The principal characters do exist, but perhaps not in the *specific* manner in which they are presented. Curiously, a few of the main characters' experiences turned out to be more common than I had previously believed. When the first incarnation of this manuscript was produced, I received communication from several families with proof that they, too, had begun their lives in this country with the very same kind of history as that of my friends.

At the end of this book (and don't read ahead!) I decided to add a "Where Are They Now?" section, which I think you will enjoy. And before *you* ask . . . yes . . . for the most part, it will be true!

Andy Andrews
Orange Beach, Alabama

PART
ONE

CHAPTER 1

IT IS EARLY SUMMER AS I SIT AT MY DESK AND FINALLY begin the process of sorting what I know to be true from what I merely suspect. As I form the words and type them into record, I shall endeavor to separate facts from the legend and myth in which they have now been shrouded for decades.

As an author, I usually have a particular work living in my head—complete with its title, plot, subplots, and ending—for months before leaping, as fully formed as I can make it, onto the page. At present, however, I haven't even a working title for this manuscript. The book you are holding, if indeed it has come to that, was nothing I ever intended to write. My next two books have been outlined and are ready to begin, but I have become distracted by an attempt to solve a mystery literally thrust into my life by the earth itself. Let me explain . . .

I live with my wife, Polly, and our two boys on a small island situated along the Florida/Alabama coastline of the northern Gulf of Mexico. There is a single, small bridge connecting us to the mainland. Orange Beach, Alabama, just to our west, is where we bank, vote, attend church, and shop for groceries.

Perdido Key, Florida, is to the east. A thirty-second drive from the bridge in that direction crosses the Florida state line and passes the world-renowned Flora-Bama Lounge, a loosely constructed conglomeration of wood, brick, and tent material most famous, I suppose, for being famous. Therefore, it is always packed, and if the wind is right, sometimes late at night I can hear strains of "Redneck Mother" or "You Don't Have to Call Me Darlin' . . . Darlin'" from my dock.

Over the past twenty years, this previously ignored coastline has increasingly become a prime destination for summer tourists and winter snowbirds drawn to the area by the turquoise water and dazzling white sand. The beach, one of the few in the world to be composed of only one mineral—in this case finely crushed quartz—is part of a one-hundred-mile stretch of beach that includes the Florida towns Panama City and Destin and is known as the "Miracle Strip."

Our home is situated on a dune line that rises twenty-five feet from the water's edge and runs east to west, affording a view of the water on both sides of the island. The landscaping is minimal at best. Here and there we've managed to coax a few flowers out of the sand, and several potted palms grace the dock. Polly holds with the belief that "natural is better," and I, having not forgotten the chores thrust upon me by my garden-crazy parents, am happy to agree.

So, instead of grass demanding to be mowed and azalea bushes begging to be fertilized or pruned or have pine straw placed by hand around their precious roots, we have sea oats and wax myrtles and ancient oak trees growing in the sand. And they grow quite nicely without any help from me. Most of the time.

Last September, I noticed the largest wax myrtle on our property had begun to die. In the almost one hundred years of its existence, the tree had grown to well over forty feet and shaded an area the size of a tennis court. It crowned the top of the dune near our kitchen porch, and boaters often noticed this magnificent monarch even before they saw the house. Because of its height and close proximity, my family was keenly aware of the tree's impending demise.

By the new year, no semblance of life was left in its branches. I was surprised to find myself strangely relieved, as if an old friend had finally passed away after a struggle that had become too difficult to witness. And after a proper period of what I called mourning and my wife termed "yard work procrastination," I knew it was time to remove the tree.

The wax myrtle, also known as the southern bayberry, was used by the Indians and early American colonists to make candles. Its distinctive, fragrant scent comes from volatile oils contained in tiny glands on the leaves. These oils render the tree highly flammable and remain in the tree long after it dies. Dead wood infused with combustible resin is not a good combination when it is located so near a house, and so it was with a heavy heart (and a portable radio tuned to the NFL play-offs) that I struck my first blow against the trunk of the tree.

I am an ax man. Ever since, as a teenager, I saw the movie in which a chainsaw was the weapon of choice, I've never been especially keen on that particular sound. So, instead of a quick rip and a crash, it took until early afternoon to chop down the tree and haul its scattered pieces away, leaving only the stump as a reminder that anything had been there at all. But as much as we loved the tree, no one wanted the reminder. "Dig it up," my wife urged in what she felt was an encouraging voice, and I did.

Granted, when surrounded by sand, a stump is not the formidable opponent it becomes when its roots have embedded themselves in clay or a rocky soil. There is, however, something to be said for a root system having spent a hundred years in search of nourishment. Tremendous mats of stringy, underground branches stretched in far larger networks than their leafy counterparts had ever accomplished in the sunshine. I was shocked and exhausted, I had a hole in the ground the size of my grandfather's Buick, and I was starting to think in regard to my dear wife, *What she doesn't know won't hurt her*. I was about to reverse course and hide the roots that were left by covering up the whole mess when my shovel struck something that didn't feel like root.

For a brief moment, the shovel stuck. It was as if I had hit a monstrous wad of gum or taffy. And the sound was different. I had grown accustomed to the high-pitched *swish* of the steel shovel as it cut through the sand, but this tone reverberated as a dull *thunk*. At the time, I didn't think it sounded like metal, but that's exactly what it was.

With the shovel's retreat, I exposed a hand-sized portion of rusted . . . something. Sand poured into a slit in the object that had obviously been opened by the slicing of the shovel. On my hands and knees, I quickly pulled wads of tiny roots away from the item and, with my fingers, pried it loose. It was a can.

I turned the heavily rusted object over in my hands, being especially careful not to cut myself on any of the sharp edges. It was large . . . like the gallon-sized cans a restaurant uses for vegetables or refills of ketchup. The can was sealed at both ends, but the rust, I noticed, had created several tiny holes in its surface in addition to the large one made by the shovel's blow.

The presence of the holes made it apparent that the can was not filled with food or liquid of any kind, but still, it was heavier than an empty can should feel. And it rattled when I turned it. Although I assumed the clatter to be caused by shells and sand, I was curious and pried apart the thin, fragile metal.

Inside the can, dank and mildewed, was what I determined to be an old chamois— once soft leather now stiffened by age and the rusty dampness in which it had been imprisoned. Pulling the leather free from the can, I saw that it had, at one time, been carefully folded. Now, though, it was shrunken somewhat, blackened by mold and almost hard on its edges like a big, ugly potholder that someone had starched.

The leather folds came apart easily in my hands, and as they did, a button fell out and onto the sand at my knees. A silver button. Though somewhat tarnished, the face of the button was beautifully etched with an anchor. From its back

extended a single loop surrounded by let-
ters so tiny that I was unable to make out anything more
than a *K*, an *R*, and on down the line of script, what I
thought might be an *A*.

Placing the button on the kitchen porch behind me, I
tugged harder at the leather from which it had come and
tore a piece completely off. Three more buttons, identical to

the first, along with a ring, fell into the sand. The ring was also silver, a bit more discolored than the buttons, and had as its center point an eagle surrounded by a wreath. The ring also had letters—these much larger—which ran the entire outside circumference of the circle. I read the words aloud: "Wir Fahren Gegen Engelland."

Not being able to translate or even identify the language, I set the ring aside with the buttons and continued to peel apart the crusty leather. With the final layer laid open, I slowly set the chamois on the sand and gazed open-mouthed at what it held. There were four more buttons, making a total of eight, a silver anchor badge about 2 inches tall by 1 ½ inches wide, some kind of black-and-silver medal with a bit of red, black, and white ribbon attached, and three, only slightly water-damaged, black-and-white photographs.

The first photograph was a simple head and upper body shot of a man in military attire. I didn't recognize the uniform, but saw immediately that the buttons in the picture were the same ones I now had in my possession. In fact, I counted them. Eight silver anchor buttons in the photo . . . and eight on my porch. I really couldn't tell if the man in the picture was twenty or forty, and in that way, he reminded me of old pictures I have seen of college kids in the nineteen thirties or forties. They all looked years older than they actually were.

The man was not smiling. It was as if he was not entirely comfortable with the idea of having a photograph made. He was not thin or fat, though "thick" might have been an accurate description of his body type. The same eagle that appeared on the ring was also on display on the right breast of his uniform jacket and the top of an odd, beret-type cap. Stitched in large, Gothic script along the lower brim of the cap was the word *Kriegsmarine*.

The second photograph was smaller and had a decorative black border framing the print. In it were three figures: a young woman in what struck me as the best dress she owned, a man in a suit and white shirt with no tie, and a baby in a wagon between them. Whether the child was a boy or girl, I couldn't tell. Though the woman looked directly (fearfully?) into the camera, the man's attention was focused toward the child, causing his face to appear in profile. I wasn't certain, but I thought that maybe he was the same uniformed man in the previous photograph.

It was the third photograph, in addition to the ribboned medal, that had my attention. The black-and-silver military decoration was cast in the shape of a cross. At the bottom leg of the cross was a date, 1939, and in its center a more familiar symbol. I blinked as I touched it with my finger and shivered, whether from the January chill or something unseen, I didn't know.

. Quickly I looked again to the last photograph. Men on a boat of some sort . . . lined up as if for inspection. On the right corner of the front line, yes, there was the uniformed man from the first picture. Four officers in highly decorated military overcoats were in the foreground of the shot. Three wore dark clothing with what I imagined to be gold or silver

trim. The fourth man, to the far left of the photograph, was dressed immaculately in an outfit cut in the same design, but of a paler material. It was this man whose face I recognized. This was the man for whom the symbol on the medal had been created. But why on earth was a picture of Adolf Hitler buried in my backyard?

CHAPTER 2

A WEEK LATER, I WAS STILL NO CLOSER TO ANSWERING MY question. Where had this stuff come from? At least the Internet, with its various search engines, had begun to fill in some of the blanks about what the actual pieces were. And the swastika embossed on the medal gave me some idea of what I might find.

After rushing inside and fanning out the items on the kitchen table for my astonished wife, I retreated to my office and cranked up the computer. The first word I searched was *Kriegsmarine,* the script on the man's hat in the first picture. I quickly found that it was the name of the German navy controlled by the Nazi regime until 1945. Previously titled the Reichsmarine, the Kriegsmarine was formed in May of 1935 after Germany passed the "Law for the Reconstruction of the National Defense Force." This law brought back into existence a German military presence that had been essentially banned by the Treaty of Versailles at the end of World War I.

I next typed in *Kriegsmarine buttons* and was instantly rewarded. There, on my computer screen, was an enlargement, front and back view, of a button exactly like the eight in my possession. The front of the button proudly displayed the anchor while the magnification of the back side clearly revealed the word *Kriegsmarine* stamped in a semicircle. Remembering the letters I had barely made out on the back of the first button I found, I dug an old 8X photographer's loupe out of my desk and looked at the back of one of the actual buttons. There it was, the same semicircular engraving of the same word that stared back at me from the computer.

As I moved my eye from the magnification device, I noticed that the photographer's loupe—a small plastic piece with the brand name Lupe—had an engraving of its own. "Made in Germany," it said. If it hadn't been so weird, I would have laughed out loud.

The medal—easy to find—was an Iron Cross. First instituted by King Friedrich of Prussia in 1813, it was adopted as a piece of political imagery by Adolf Hitler during the opening hours of World War II and became the most recognizable decoration to be won by a member of the German military. The Iron Cross was awarded for bravery in the face of the enemy. The actual medal itself was seldom worn, but often carried. An Iron Cross recipient usually displayed only the brightly colored ribbon by running it out the top right buttonhole of his jacket. In the first photograph, I could see that very piece of red, white, and black cloth featured prominently on the Kriegsmariner's uniform.

Next, I began a frustrating search for the *silver anchor badge* by typing in those exact words. After trying *German silver anchor badge, German silver rope anchor badge,* and *German Navy silver rope anchor badge* with no luck, I substituted the words *pin* and *medal* for *badge, Nazi* for *German, Kriegsmarine* for *Navy,* and every combination of those terms I could concoct, with the same results. Nothing.

Pausing for a moment, I sat back and stared at the badge/pin/medal/whatever on my desk. I had literally scanned the pictures of more than one hundred German decorations and military awards, but hadn't come close to anything resembling this impressive piece of masculine jewelry. Picking it up, I placed the silver badge on the gray background of my laptop. Then, I saw something that, unbelievably, had escaped my attention. On the left side of the pin, from the anchor's flange at the bottom to its cross bar at the top, rested a large *U*. Matching it on the right side was a *B* of equal dimension. Both letters appeared as mere decorative support, so I reassured myself I wasn't a total idiot for having overlooked them. But now that I *did* see them, it was as if I could see nothing else—like the optical puzzles that, when you finally see the picture, you wonder how you could have ever missed it in the first place.

U B . . . I wondered. My eyes narrowed. U-boat? Immediately I typed in *Kriegsmarine U-boat silver anchor badge* and got the hit that led me to a picture of the badge in my possession. Subsequent searches using several different search engines finally gave me a fairly complete background on the medal.

Interestingly, it was commissioned by the German government in 1910 and worn at that time by officers in the submarine corps. For some reason, the Nazi regime chose not to include the medal in its official notices of recognition. Thus, I found that this particular design was worn by several U-boat officers during World War II as a deniable way of protesting Hitler and his policies. These officers, who either inherited the badge from a relative or had a copy made by a jeweler, considered themselves Germans, not Nazis—a curious but apparently not uncommon distinction.

The U-boat connection also led me to a picture and history of the ring. The engraving, *Wir Fahren Gegen Engelland,* translated "We sail against England." Under close examination, again with the loupe, I could see a swastika in the eagle's talons, all set on top of a tiny submarine, surrounded by a wreath. The written information about the ring was specific: it was worn only by an officer of the Unterseebootwaffe—the German submarine force. But who? The man in the first picture? And still the question lingered . . . why was it abandoned and buried here?

After I identified all the items, I turned my attention to the final photograph—the one with Hitler. Three additional officers appeared in the picture with the man most sane people still consider the sheer embodiment of evil. The officer standing immediately to the Führer's left, pointing at something unseen, was in shadow, but by comparing pictures and searching Kriegsmarine files online, I soon identified him as Admiral Karl Doenitz, commander of Hitler's U-boat fleet, later commander in chief of the Kriegsmarine.

I was never able to match a picture with the second officer who stands just behind and to the left of Doenitz or the third officer, of whom one can see only his head. I could only determine, with observational techniques honed by years of watching detective shows on television, that one of them seemed old and fat while the other appeared young and handsome.

"THIS IS A LITTLE GIRL."

I looked up from my book. Polly was holding the picture of the man and woman with the baby in the wagon. Sitting at the other end of the couch with her feet in my lap, my wife had just stuffed another pillow behind her back and was drinking a cup of tea as she gazed at the photograph.

"What makes you think that?" I asked. Having attached little significance to that particular picture, I had given it a cursory examination at best and certainly had not attempted to guess the sex of the child. "Why do you say 'girl'?"

She placed the cup on the small table beside her and sighed softly. "It just is. It's a baby girl. The mom looks so sad."

I was quiet. The boys were at their grandmother's, and Polly and I were spending the weekend alone. It had rained constantly—a slow, foggy, winter drizzle that hangs on the coast sometimes for days. We had not turned on the television a single time, choosing instead to read or talk by the fireplace in our bedroom. The conversation had turned frequently to one or another of the items that had been buried under the old wax myrtle. Polly, for some reason, had taken the photograph with the child and used it as a bookmark. Several times, when she didn't think I was looking, I caught her frowning as she stared at the simple, but somewhat odd, picture.

I had long ago learned to trust my wife's intuition. Her perceptions about people, their feelings or intentions, were uncannily accurate. That is not to say I understood or always agreed completely with her conclusions; however, more than a few times I had been stunned by the precise detail she was able to discern.

I closed my book and eased it to the floor. Polly continued to hold the photograph, but stared out the rain-streaked window. "Dear," I said softly. "What's happening in that picture? Try to imagine it for me."

She didn't look at me, but pushed a lock of dark hair

from her eyes and began to speak. "They are a family . . . a young family. The man and woman have been married a short time. This is their first child . . ." Polly cut her eyes at me. "And it *is* a girl. I don't know why I'm so sure of that, but I am." I nodded, urging her to continue.

"The man is the same man in the first photo . . . the guy in the uniform . . . so this is a picture that was made before he left for the war." She paused and took a deep breath. "The woman is very sad . . . she's scared. Her baby is less than a year old, and she doesn't think they'll ever see the man again." Polly was quiet for a moment, then added, "I don't think they did."

IT RAINED FOR THE REST OF THE MORNING AND INTO THE afternoon. After lunch, I had gone to the dock alone and, under the covered area, lit one of the Mexican firepots. Warming my hands, I studied the blaze and reflected on Polly's thoughts about the family in the photograph. Her words had left me unsettled. I couldn't get any of it off my mind, and my work was beginning to suffer. I had already fielded several calls from my publisher and business manager about "the next book." "How is the manuscript coming?" they wanted to know as the date of my next deadline was politely worked into the conversation. "Great," I lied. "In fact, let me get off the phone and get back to work."

In actuality, I hadn't even begun. The two books I had been so excited about a week earlier had faded deeply into the recesses of the procrastination depot in my brain. The couple or three times I had attempted to write, my mind wandered so madly as to render my powers of concentration virtually nonexistent. Again and again, one basic question gnawed at me and refused to let go: How had all these items come to be hidden here, of all places?

Without warning, an idea of enormously obvious proportions popped into my mind. Why hadn't I used the Internet to explore a possible connection between the Gulf of Mexico and the Kriegsmarine? Quickly I put out the fire while shaking my head at the awesome ability I seem to possess that allows me to overlook the apparent.

Moments later, in my office, I connected to Google and typed in *German U-boats in Gulf of Mexico*. Less than a second later, I was staring wide-eyed at the results of the search. There were 1,940 hits on the topic I'd requested. I couldn't believe it.

I clicked on the first Web site and read the first sentence. It said, "During the years 1942 and 1943, a fleet of over twenty German U-boats cruised the Gulf of Mexico seeking to disrupt the vital flow of oil carried by tankers from U.S. ports."

I swallowed hard and read the second sentence. "The U-boats succeeded in sending fifty-six vessels to the bottom; thirty-nine of these are in the state waters of Texas, Louisiana, and Florida."

Furiously I clicked on site after site, each adding to or confirming the information of the last. In fact, the only discrepancy I could find was the number of merchant ships the U-boats sank. I was convinced, however, that the true number, depending upon which source I believed, was between fifty-six and sixty-two. And remember, those were only in the Gulf of Mexico.

Reading more, I was astounded to learn that when the Atlantic coast was included, only a handful of U-boats had sunk 397 ships—and that was in the first six months of

1942 alone! Eventually, before Hitler called them back, the U-boats destroyed more than 800 vessels in American waters. Unbelievably, many of those were within sight of people on the beach.

Cape Hatteras in North Carolina became known as "Torpedo Junction" as bodies and cargo began to float in. On May 4, 1942, sunbathers in Boca Raton, Florida, watched in horror as the U-564 surfaced and torpedoed the tanker *Eclipse* in broad daylight and in full view of the beach. The German submarine then turned and blasted the freighter *Delisle* and her cargo of camouflage paint. The subsequent explosions and shock waves rumbled over the panicked tourists on the beach with a deafening roar.

Explosions and burning wrecks, all along the eastern seaboard and Gulf coast, were regularly seen at night. Dead men, debris, and oil began to wash ashore, and still, America did not institute the blackouts that were in effect along the coasts of England and Germany. Even when the merchant ships turned out their own lights, the U-boats had only to surface and use the background of the U.S. coast-line—whose lights could be seen for more than twenty-five miles—to target the huge vessels.

What was the cost in lives? I wondered. The answer was easily found. During less than a two-year period, more than 1,300 navy men, 201 Coast Guard personnel, and exactly 5,682 merchant marines lost their lives due to U-boat attacks *in American waters!*

Now I had another question: Why had I never heard about this? It was all undoubtedly true. There was too much documentation. The information exists in droves on the Internet, in hundreds of thousands of old newspaper files, and in well over two hundred books on the subject. So . . .

why was I so ignorant about this astonishingly recent period in my nation's history? More to the point, why had *everyone* seemingly forgotten?

During dinner, as I laid out everything I had learned, Polly sat quietly and listened, occasionally shaking her head in wonder at the facts that were "news" to her as well. Then, in response to the question, "Where do I go from here?" she gave me a practical answer.

"Ask the old people," she said.

CHAPTER 3

THE ORANGE BEACH/PERDIDO KEY AREA OF THE northern Gulf of Mexico was virtually uninhabited during World War II—at least the beach itself had no permanent homes. Fishermen and their families lived inland, within access of the Gulf. They built houses where they could dock their boats—on the bays and coastal rivers—and except for a weekend cottage or two, there were no structures at all close to the unpredictable waves of the Gulf. Those dwellings that did exist were set back in the dunes, far from the beach, and were usually more than a mile from each other.

Highway 3 (now Highway 59) from Foley, Alabama, ran due south to the water's edge while County Roads 180, 182, and 292 generally paralleled the beach from Fort Morgan at the mouth of Mobile Bay to the Pensacola Sound. Most of the area's population at that time worked close to home, shrimping, fishing, or farming, but a few drove east or west every morning to newly created jobs in the defense industry. Brookley Field was on the outskirts of Mobile, and the Pensacola Naval Air Station marked the eastern boundary of Perdido Key.

Lois Metcalf has lived by herself since her husband died

nine years ago. In the tiny community of Lillian, she sits on her back porch every morning and looks out over Perdido Bay. She is a small woman, and her hair is dyed a shockingly dark shade for a person of her age—what my wife calls "Loretta Lynn black." I was referred to Mrs. Metcalf by several of our mutual friends. "She grew up here," they said, "and can tell you everything you'd need to know about the history of the area."

She was twelve years old in 1942, she told me. Then she grinned and admonished me about doing the math in my head. I liked her immediately. I asked her if she knew anything about German U-boats in the Gulf during World War II. Her daddy was a shrimper, she told me in a strong voice, and she remembered him grumbling about a particular commercial fisherman whom he suspected of selling fuel and food to "Nazi subs." She pronounced the word "Natsey."

"Did he ever find out if it was true?" I asked.

"No," she replied, "and I know that for sure . . . 'cause he'da shot him if he had." Then she added, "My daddy was just that way, you know." I nodded as if, indeed, I did.

I was about to ask her if she knew anything else, rumors even, when she volunteered some new information. "We all hated them sneaky Nazi submariners. When they sunk them boys from Mobile, that was it."

"What was this?" I asked. "When?"

"End of February, 1942," she said. "It was a freighter. Beautiful ship named after Mobile . . . the SS *Azalea City*. We all went down to the docks to cheer her out of port. Lots of local boys manning her. My older sister went to a dance with one of 'em, as I recall. Anyhow, the Nazis stuck a torpedo in her off Ocean City somewhere. Maryland, you know? We heard about it a week after it happened.

Killed every man on board. More'n thirty of 'em, seems it was."

She was right. According to several Internet sources I checked as soon as I got home, the SS *Azalea City* was torpedoed by a German U-boat on February 20, 1942. She went down with thirty-eight crew. There were no survivors.

During the following week, I talked with Mr. Fern Cottrall and Mr. Hollis Parker—both residents of the Baldwin County Nursing Home. I also spent a great deal of time with Mr. and Mrs. Halkman, the parents of a local fireman, and Barton and Frances Dale, a couple who volunteer at the local library. All were at least in their seventies and had interesting stories about U-boats, German agents, and mined harbor entrances. This group provided nothing verifiable or new, however. Add those unproductive sessions to my unease at the certainty Mr. Cottrall displayed about German submarines still stalking the Gulf, still sinking ships, and due to invade Florida any day, and you will get some idea of my frustration at the time. In addition, he repeatedly called me Carl.

The next Monday morning, Mrs. Theresa Larson and her son, James, who appeared to be sixty-something or so, sat on the dock and had coffee with Polly and me. Mrs. Larson and her first husband (for some reason I did not write his name down in my notes) often camped on the beach during those years with their young family. On two consecutive evenings, during the hot calm of the full moon in July 1942, the entire family saw a submarine surface. While it was some distance offshore, Mrs. Larson insisted they were able to see the outline of the U-boat quite clearly in the moonlight.

And what's more, she told us, on the second night, men

came out of the sub's tower and entered the water to swim. She assured me that, with the breeze in their favor, she and her husband heard the splashing and laughter—along with a few German words—quite clearly. Her son, James, told us that while he must have been too young to remember the incident, it was the same story his father had told until he died.

Though there was no specific proof of what Mrs. Larson claimed, I did uncover anecdotal evidence in several of the Kriegsmarine diaries available to historians that shows evidence of U-boat crews often being allowed out on calm nights for fresh air and a swim.

Kingston Monroe, known to everyone as "Mr. King," works as a greeter at the South Baldwin Regional Medical Center. He is still tall and ramrod straight, but snow-white hair and blotchy skin give evidence of the eighty-something years he has lived. I met him for lunch at Chicken & Seafood, my favorite restaurant just south of the hospital in Foley, which serves—surprise—chicken and seafood. Mr. King filled in quite a few blanks about what people knew and thought back then.

"Early '42," he began, "or at least by the spring of . . . ever'body was talking about U-boats. Them that hadn't seen one in person, or at least heard them jokers out in the dark, knew somebody who had. Now, for sure, I know all these folks wadn' seeing 'em. But just as for sure, they was there. And they was gettin' fuel somewheres too."

Now came the question I really wanted to ask: "Mr. King, do you think any of the U-boat crews ever came ashore?"

He rolled his eyes and looked at me like I was crazy. "Well, son, what do you think? There wadn' no potato chip machines in them things, and they weren't gassin' up every Monday morning in Berlin!" I chuckled politely as he took a deep breath. "Listen here, you look it up, the navy boys captured one sub and got into it before the Nazis could scuttle her. There was Campbell's Soup cans in the galley . . . and a big box of fresh turnip greens." I raised my eyebrows, and the old man looked pleased that he'd obviously told me something I hadn't heard.

Then he cocked his head, smiled, and leaned closer. "And I'll tell you somethin' else. Don't matter now noways. Several of them German boys, when they yanked 'em out of the U-boat, had ticket stubs from the Saenger Theatre in their pockets." He studied my surprised expression for a beat or two, then added, "Yep. The Saenger Theatre. That'd be North Rampart Street in downtown New Orleans."

Mr. King smiled as I scribbled furiously in my notebook. "Course you won't find anything in the history books about that particular little event."

Sheesh, I thought, *I couldn't find anything about any of this in history books!* Glancing up, I asked the obvious question anyway. "Why not?"

"'Cause nobody knew. Navy boy from Elberta told me. Bernard Hanson. Bernie's dead now, but he told me. Things was differ'nt back then, son. The government was keeping it quiet as they could. They figured if we knew the Nazis was ashore and mingling with us—hey, folks'd be shootin' ever' blue-eyed stranger that came to town. Probably a good thing. Not to tell, I mean."

I agreed with him, talked a bit more, paid for our meal, thanked Mr. King, and left. I did check some records to which I had access through a United States Navy source. Mr. King was correct. The items found in the U-boat are still on file at the Pentagon. For some reason, however, after all these years, that specific U-boat's number is still classified and not even available through the Freedom of Information Act. But with my own eyes, I saw the four ticket stubs from the Saenger. They are preserved in heavy lamination and rest on an admiral's desk at Annapolis. By the way, in case you are curious . . . the soup was tomato.

My most meaningful contact came about quite by chance really. We were leaving church one Sunday morning, me with our younger boy in my arms, when I happened into Mr. and Mrs. Newman. They have been members of Orange Beach United Methodist Church since the congregation began meeting in a doublewide trailer years ago. The Newmans appeared to be in their eighties, maybe older, and he had been a commercial fisherman in his younger years.

As strange as it may seem to call an old couple "cute," everyone agrees they are exactly that. He calls her "Mrs. Newman," and she calls him just plain "Newman." They are among the nicest, most popular people in the church. I rarely see them together that they are not holding hands. She is always laughing and smiling, while Mr. Newman, also jovial and quick to tease, is quite a hit with the kids. He carries candy and gum in his pockets, and my boys, especially, love him.

After saying hello and allowing time for the children to collect their usual favorite (root beer lollipops), I realized that, for whatever reason, I had neglected to talk to the Newmans about my latest obsession. Both had been supposed pioneers of the area, I knew, and were favorite people of mine so, less careful than I was with someone I didn't know, I blurted out a quick question: "Hey, do you two know anything about German U-boats in the Gulf during

World War II?" They continued to look at the boys, and thinking they had not heard me, I started to ask the question again when Mrs. Newman fixed me with her usual smile. "Why in the world do you ask that, Andy?"

I shrugged. "I found some stuff—pictures and buttons. Anyway, I'm just doing some research."

"Writing a book?"

"I don't really know yet. It's more a novelty than anything else at this point. But I gotta tell you, I am somewhat amazed that most people do not seem to remember this . . . You and Mr. Newman lived here then, didn't you?" She nodded, and we looked at her husband, who had kneeled and was playing with my children. I asked again: "What do you know about all that?"

She put her hand on her husband's shoulder. Still looking at me, she said, "Well, Newman knows a lot about it, but nobody wants to listen to our old stories anymore."

"I do," I replied.

Mr. Newman stood as his wife invited me for coffee the next day. "You'll tell Andy some stories, won't you, honey?" she asked him.

"Sure, if you want to listen," he said to me as we shook hands and walked toward the church parking lot. "Course my memory ain't what it used to be . . . what was your name again?" I raised my eyebrows, and he chuckled at his own joke. "Nine in the morning okay with you?"

I ARRIVED AT THEIR HOUSE THE NEXT MORNING PROMPTLY ON the hour. At the end of a tree-lined street, the Newmans lived in one of Foley's older neighborhoods. They had moved away from the water more than a decade earlier when he sold his fishing boat and, with a tidy profit from the bay-front property that had been theirs since 1948, bought this three-bedroom brick home for cash on his seventieth birthday.

Familiar with the place, I stepped from my vehicle and ventured over to the edge of the driveway to look at the famous Newman blueberry bushes. They were bare now, but in late spring would be loaded with the tiny, luscious fruit. And then would come the packs of kids, mine included, who picked from the bushes, stuffing more berries into their mouths than into the buckets they held. Neither of the Newmans ever ate a berry—stained their dentures, they claimed—but both of them watered and fertilized those bushes as if their lives depended on it.

I climbed the steps to the porch where Polly and I had sat many times, eating sandwiches and drinking sweet iced tea with the older couple while our boys gorged themselves with ripe blueberries. Mrs. Newman met me at the front door. Her hair was the gray-blue color I had seen on many older women, and the dress she wore was awash with bright pink and dark red triangles. I had never seen a picture of her as a young woman, but it was easy enough to imagine. She was still beautiful.

"Come on in," she said, holding the door open. "You like lots of sugar in your coffee, don't you." She stated it as a fact, not as a question.

"Yes, ma'am, with cream . . . and could you put some extra caffeine in it?" I teased.

She laughed politely and led me into the kitchen where Mr. Newman waited. He rose from his seat at the breakfast table as I entered the room. About five ten or so in brown work pants and a plaid flannel shirt, he still had the ruddy complexion of a man who had spent his life outdoors.

Extending his hand, he greeted me. "Sit down, sit down. I got ahead of you on the coffee. It's the only thing keeping my heart beating, I think."

"That and me, you old man," Mrs. Newman said with a cackle, which prompted her husband to grin and wink at me. After pouring more coffee for him and a first cup for me, Mrs. Newman sat down at the table with us. She moved her chair to face me and eased her left hand into his right.

"At church yesterday," Mrs. Newman began, "you mentioned you found some things . . . buttons and photographs, I believe you said. Photographs of what?"

I answered their questions—they were mostly *her* questions—and before long, I was afforded two unexpected surprises. One, they were extremely computer literate, something seldom seen in people of their generation. And two, they knew more about the subject of U-boats in the Gulf of Mexico than anyone with whom I had been able to speak.

Mr. Newman brought out a cardboard box of files printed from Web sites and copied from library books. He showed me a list of every American vessel sunk by U-boats during the war, their tonnage, location, and crew numbers. He answered questions that, frankly, I had not thought to ask. I was shocked at the average age of a U-boat crew (just twenty years old) and amazed at the conditions they endured.

Mr. Newman allowed me to examine written accounts by crew members of torpedoed tankers and freighters. The versions varied wildly according to the ship and the teller of the tale. Some stories were bitter narratives by survivors of sunken vessels whose crews had been savagely machine-gunned from their lifeboats by the U-boat that had torpedoed their ship, then surfaced in their midst. Others carefully recorded accounts of U-boats allowing the crew members to row away from their doomed ship before it was sunk. Then, in amazement, they watched as the U-boat's officers emerged from the conning tower only to give them food, water, and compass bearings toward land.

"There was a difference between a German and a Nazi," Mr. Newman stated. "The Kriegsmarine had a lot of Germans . . . not so many Nazis." I frowned. Honestly it was not a distinction I had ever made. Noting my confusion and perhaps interpreting it as disbelief, the old man said, "You see a difference between Americans and the Ku Klux Klan, don't you?" I nodded. "Well, there you go." I was silent for a moment, while he wiped his face roughly with his hand.

Mrs. Newman interrupted. "While I never actually saw a U-boat," she said, "I talked to a few who did. Newman and I have always been curious about this period in history. The submarines were here. They were in the Gulf, though it seems no one remembers. In any case, we became curious about the men. Obviously—I mean, read the accounts of the sinkings—more than occasionally there were compassionate men in positions of leadership."

"The Kriegsmarine," Mr. Newman said, "and specifically the U-boat service, was an area in the German military where a vessel's crew was generally able to think and act as smaller, individual entities. The captain was law, and whatever he ordered was carried out. Therefore, if the ship's officers were decent men, the crew behaved and dealt with their enemies in a decent way . . . that is to say, at least, they fought under the rules of the Geneva Convention . . . none of this shooting helpless men in the water. In the Gulf, a U-boat crew was two thousand miles from the High Command, and though there were Nazi party officials on every boat and ship, the officers and crews, for the most part, considered themselves German— not Nazi—and didn't hold the same sadistic beliefs as Hitler and his cronies."

The second time we got together, Polly and I met with the Newmans at Wolf Bay Lodge, a favorite lunch place in nearby Elberta. I had more questions to ask, and Mrs. Newman wanted to see the items I had uncovered beneath the tree. Between bites of fried oyster sandwiches and crab claws and sips of sweet iced tea, we talked—mostly about the pictures. The Newmans seemed to have the same fascination about the family picture that we had, and both were curious about the Iron Cross and the U-boat officer's ring.

By my third visit, we had almost run out of things to discuss. Mr. Newman had taken ill and was not his usual jolly self. As he went to the bedroom to lie down, his wife moved me into their living room. She showed me pictures of fishing boats and satsuma groves and what the beach looked like before anyone knew what a condo was.

We sat on the couch, and she smiled as the gentle sounds of her husband's snoring drifted through the closed bedroom door. "He is a good man," she said simply.

"Yes, ma'am," I agreed with a nod. I didn't really have anything else to say.

"Day after tomorrow, we are going to Louisiana for a few weeks. Do you need to talk to us anymore?"

"Not about this, I don't think." I shrugged. "I'm sort of at a dead end. I appreciate your help, though. It's all so interesting, and yet . . ." I paused, searching for the completion of a thought I couldn't quite grasp.

"And yet what?" she prodded.

I sighed. "I guess I was hoping to wrap it all up in a neat little package."

"Life is seldom that way."

"Well, don't think I'm just finding that out." She smiled. "I was just hoping, at least, to find out where the things I found buried in our yard came from. But, I suppose, that's too much to expect. After all, it's been more than half a century." Chuckling dryly, I added, "And my wife is still concerned about the family in the picture."

Mrs. Newman reached over and patted my hand. "Things have a way of working out, son. You tell your sweet Polly that that family is fine."

"All right, I will," I said, not really convinced that it mattered. Preparing to leave, I hugged her and asked her to thank Mr. Newman for me. As it turned out, she didn't have to. He woke up as we were saying good-bye and insisted on walking me to my car.

I drove home with an uneasy feeling. Things in my life generally "came together," but this had not. Instead, I struggled with a perplexing riddle that had consumed my time, derailed my writing schedule, and was apparently unsolvable to boot. What a mess!

That night after dinner, Polly herded the boys to the bathtub while I cleaned the kitchen. When the phone rang, I answered and was surprised to hear Mrs. Newman's voice on the other end. She wanted to let me know, she said, that Newman was better.

"Thanks," I replied, somewhat curious that she would call just to relay that information, but I played along. "I'm glad to hear it. He is a great guy."

"Yes, he is." She stopped briefly as if to make up her mind about something, then continued, "Andy?"

"Yes, ma'am?"

"Have you ever been to the old Civil War fort?"

I knew she was talking about Fort Morgan. The massive old stone-and-earthworks stands on the tip of a peninsula that runs almost twenty miles due west of town. The peninsula is squeezed by the Gulf on its southern shore and the waters of Mobile Bay to the north. I answered her question. "Yes, ma'am. I've been there."

"I never mentioned this because it was only a rumor . . . Newman says I shouldn't say anything . . ." She spoke haltingly, and her voice grew faint as if she were pulling the phone away from her mouth.

"Mrs. Newman . . . ," I said.

"Yes?"

"Tell me."

"Well, people used to say a Nazi spy was shot out there . . . on the peninsula . . . that's what people used to say . . . that one was killed and buried, and no one ever found out. I just thought you might want to know."

I hung up the phone and sat down heavily in one of the kitchen chairs. "She just thought I might want to know," I said to myself out loud. My mind was spinning. *I have Nazi medals and a picture of Adolf Hitler in my backyard. German U-boats torpedoed tankers right off the coast here, and nobody remembers.* "And, oh, by the way, I think a spy *was shot down the street . . . just thought you'd want to know!"*

Shaking my head, I stood up and, before I got back to the dishes in the sink, turned to the telephone in its cradle and said, "Thanks a lot."

PART

TWO

CHAPTER 4

July 16, 1942

CAPTAIN WALTER CROSLAND GLANCED OVER HIS LEFT shoulder. The lights of Havana were still visible off the port stern. He yawned and slid his pocket watch from his pants, angling it into the glow cast by the ship's dials and gauges. It was almost three o'clock in the morning, and the freighter *Gertrude* was not yet thirty miles off the northeast coast of Cuba. Crosland reached for his cigarettes and tried to ignore the uneasiness that had tugged at him since leaving the harbor more than three hours earlier.

There were U-boats in the area. He knew it, and so did everyone else. That's why he was running at night with his lights out, something he had never done. Only three days earlier, the steamship *Oneida,* a massive 2,309-ton vessel sailing around the eastern tip of Cuba, was sent to the bottom by a pair of torpedoes that struck her in the main engine compartments. After news of that disaster filtered in, Captain Crosland had delayed his departure in hopes that the U-boat—surely there was only one—might sail away in search of more productive hunting grounds.

There was a limit, however, to the delay the *Gertrude*'s

cargo could withstand. A small freighter, she was loaded with sixteen tons of onions, among other assorted fruits and vegetables. It was food for the fighting men, Crosland knew, and as such, was fair game for the "wolves of the sea." Leery of spoilage, the captain had steered out of port at midnight, but was bound up by strong winds and heavy swells. The freighter was barely making ten knots.

The bridge door opened as Briley, his first mate and the officer on watch, came inside with a mug of steaming coffee. "Everyone's sacked out, Cap'n, and all's clear except for these seas. Still only moderate, though . . . three to four feet."

Crosland grunted acknowledgment as he accepted the coffee from the younger man. The deck pitched as he took a sip. He grimaced and said, "Well, whether I pour it all over my arms or get it down my gut, I s'pose it'll keep me awake."

Briley chuckled dutifully, then spoke. "Cap'n, will we be . . ."

Without a hint of warning, a piercing squeal followed by a loud, roaring voice washed over them. "Achtung!" The captain ducked, hunching his shoulders, while Briley involuntarily dove to the floor. "Achtung!" the voice came again. "Attention!" This time in English. Almost immediately, Crosland recognized the voice as coming from some type of loudspeaker. It rang with electronic feedback, but was clear and so obviously close that it had startled the men to the point of near panic.

Gathering his wits, Crosland grabbed the ship's wheel and desperately began turning the freighter to the starboard, away from the thundering voice. That the voice had addressed them first in German had not escaped his notice. Once more, the disembodied voice from the dark boomed across the water, again in English, this time adding another command: "Shut down your engines, and abandon your ship immediately!"

For a moment, Crosland actually considered running, but was quickly overcome by the reality of the situation. A U-boat—it was obviously a U-boat—had tracked and maneuvered ahead of him. The submarine was faster, it was armed, and it would undoubtedly destroy him if he sought to escape. Without delay, the *Gertrude*'s master palmed the button overriding the big diesels and snapped, "Briley, get the crew off."

Crosland flipped an alarm switch. A siren from within the ship began to scream in short, shrill bursts. The first mate still had not moved from the floor. "Briley, get up! Let's get this crew off!"

"Cap'n, should we . . ."

Crosland kicked the terrified man and screamed, "Get up now! They're gonna sink this ship! Get the men into the lifeboats! Go!"

As Briley ran below, Crosland exited the bridge to the outside, searching vainly for the U-boat he knew was just beyond his vision. The voice assaulted his senses once more. "Abandon your ship immediately! Abandon your ship immediately!"

Crosland slid down the stairs and met the crew emptying onto the main deck. Confusion reigned as the men frantically unbuckled the lifeboats, but within minutes, using the block and tackle, they were lowering themselves down the side of the doomed freighter. The captain was the last man off. "Pull away," Crosland ordered as the men scrambled into place and fastened oars into oarlocks. "Pull away hard!"

When Crosland's lifeboat was barely fifty yards away, he began to make out a shape and half stood, struggling against the pitching ocean, to see over the heads of the crew. Suddenly he yelled, "Pull starboard! Starboard!" The lifeboat was steering straight into the lee of the surfaced submarine.

Finally away and to the U-boat's side, the *Gertrude*'s captain called for his men to cease rowing as they all stared at the sub's long, sinister shape. It was painted completely black, and Crosland could make out the moving shapes of several men on the tower. Then, with fire that lit the night sky from a location on the deck of the sub, but beyond its tower, a huge gun opened up on the *Gertrude*. The first shell set the freighter on fire. Then, shell after shell was blasted into the superstructure of the vessel until, in less than ninety seconds, she slipped under the waves. Crosland sat down heavily, vaguely aware of the smell of burning onions.

The crew in the lifeboats watched as the U-boat, finished with its larger prey, revved its surface diesels and turned to come after them. A few of the men cried out. They had heard the stories of lifeboats and survivors being shredded by the machine guns of a victorious U-boat.

Crosland, however, still had his wits about him and was curious about the order to abandon ship. Most tankers and freighters, he knew, were simply torpedoed, the attack coming as a surprise, leaving the crew who survived to get off and into the water the best way they could. This was war. Everyone knew it, and mercy was rarely part of the equation.

As the U-boat churned closer to him and began to slow her engines, Crosland thought about the war and his part in it. He was an old man, more than fifty, and had been turned down by the navy when he'd tried to enlist. Running a merchant ship that supplied the Allies was his way of serving his country. He had not, however, really expected to see any action. Yet here he was, a moment away from what he hoped would be a quick death. *This really is a* world *war,* he thought. *I am sixty miles from Miami Beach and about to get killed by Nazis.*

The submarine settled to a stop less than thirty feet away. This time without the loudspeaker, the man from the tower shouted down, again in perfect, unaccented English: "Is your lead officer aboard?"

Crosland took a deep breath as his crew turned toward him. He stood and answered in a clear voice: "I am he."

The captain noticed the man who spoke huddling with another man wearing a white officer's cap. The speaker turned and said, "Our commander wishes to know if you have fresh water aboard."

Crosland wanted to curse him. He wanted to swim over and wring his neck, but he said simply, "No."

Quickly his answer was relayed to the man in the white cap, and two canteens were slung from the sub's tower into the lifeboat. "Do you have a compass?" he was then asked. Crosland almost wished the Germans *would* shoot. He had never felt so helpless in his life. "No," he replied.

"Look at my hand," the man commanded as he extended his arm to Crosland's left. "Your closest landfall is there. Good-bye."

"TAUCHEN," CAME THE ORDER FROM HANS GUNTHER Kuhlmann as the hatch was secured and the crew of the U-166 began to take her down. Kuhlmann was too tall by several inches to comfortably stand on the submarine's bridge, and so as not to slump more than he already did in the confining space, he removed his white cap as soon as he stepped from the ladder. The white cap was a symbol of leadership in the Unterseebootwaffe, worn only by the submarine's commander.

"Excellent work, gentlemen," Kuhlmann said to the men on the bridge. "Steady her at one hundred feet. Set a northwesterly course for one hour, at which time we will surface and resume patrol until dawn. Carry on." Orders given, the young commander retreated to his tiny room behind the bridge and pulled shut the only privacy curtain on board.

At twenty-eight years of age, Commander Kuhlmann was the second oldest man aboard. He was from Cologne, a city on Germany's eastern border, and had studied French and English—receiving higher marks in English—as a teenager. After high school, young Hans entered Germany's military service as a naval cadet and soon went to sea as an officer cadet.

Throughout the 1930s as Germany lumbered yet again toward war, Kuhlmann served as a torpedo officer aboard various gunships until being assigned to the new U-boat fleet in 1940. He served as an officer of the U-37 for fourteen months, during which time the submarine completed eight missions and sank an incredible forty-six Allied vessels. He was the Unterseebootwaffe's rising star, and early in 1942, Hans Gunther Kuhlmann was appointed commander of Germany's newest Type IXC submarine, the U-166.

"Sir?" The voice was accompanied by a sharp knock on the bulkhead outside Kuhlmann's tiny stateroom.

"Come."

The curtain was briefly pulled aside as Under-Lieutenant

Josef Bartels Landermann entered and closed it behind him. "Sit, Landermann," Kuhlmann barked roughly, loud enough to be heard beyond the curtain despite the interior noises of a sub under way.

The under-lieutenant, officially Oberfahnrich zur See, was a man somewhat shorter than his commander. At about five feet ten or eleven inches, he was powerfully built and had a plain but pleasant face framed with closely cropped brown hair. He sat as he had been ordered to do. Since Kuhlmann occupied the only chair in the cramped space, the under-lieutenant parked himself on the commander's bunk.

For several seconds, the men stared at each other, Kuhlmann glowering fiercely. Then, as if a switch had been turned, each broke into a broad grin. Stifling laughter, Kuhlmann propelled himself from the chair to the bunk and slapped the other man on the back. "You were marvelous, Josef," he whispered gleefully. "Allied supplies destroyed, not a man lost to either ship. A perfect encounter. And your English is incredible."

Nodding, but neglecting to smile, Landermann asked quietly, "Did you see the faces of their men as we swung the boat? They were certain we intended to shoot them."

Kuhlmann's joyful expression faded as he ran a hand through his thick black hair. "Yes, it has happened enough times that they expect it now. But it will not happen on this boat. War is one thing. Murder is quite another."

Each man paused briefly, contemplating that distinct difference, until Landermann broke the silence. Leaning toward the commander, he whispered conspiratorially, "So . . . what now . . . into the Gulf of Mexico?"

Kuhlmann furrowed his brow. "Of course," he replied

and, holding up a finger, added, "but not a word. Remember, you are not supposed to know."

Indeed he was not. The mission of the U-166, including its destination, was a secret to be held only by the submarine's commander and its official, onboard Nazi Party observer, a man named Ernst Schneider. But there was another secret on this submarine, one that, had the German High Command known, would have meant certain redeployment, perhaps even discipline for Kuhlmann and Landermann. The commander and his under-lieutenant had been best friends for years.

It was a situation never tolerated by the Nazi military machine, whose entire structure was based on loyalty to the Führer and mistrust of everyone else. It was dangerous to the well-being of the High Command for two men to trust each other. Before long, it was assumed, these men would begin to confide in each other and question orders—maybe even the philosophy behind those orders.

Control was ensured by means of informants carefully placed at the grassroots level throughout the military. For all appearances, they were ordinary soldiers or sailors and existed in addition to official informers—the Nazi Party observers who were placed on each U-boat and ship. These men were specifically charged to ferret out troops disloyal to the party ideal. It quickly became apparent to the High Command that it was not even necessary to place these informers with every company as long as the fighting men did not know each other well. The threat of who *might* be an informer was enough.

Josef Bartels Landermann was twenty-six. Two years younger than Kuhlmann, he was also from Cologne. The two men had been fast friends since before they were teenagers. They had grown up in the same neighborhood, gone to the same schools, and been in each other's weddings. It was only as adults that their paths diverged.

While Hans Kuhlmann intended the military as a career from the time he left high school, Josef Landermann continued his formal education on full scholarship to Oxford, in England. Intending to become a teacher, he was a student of world history, but had a gift for languages that left his professors dumbfounded. His ear for sound and nuance made Josef a popular student, for he was able to mimic any voice, any inflection, almost without exception.

Having heard a particular professor's stiff British accent every day for some time, Josef once stood up before the man arrived, walked to his desk, and impersonated him perfectly for a full minute, including the man's mannerisms and walk. Moments later, after Josef's impromptu performance had ended, the professor himself entered the classroom and began his usual routine . . . only this time to uproarious laughter.

Returning from Oxford, Josef married Tatiana, his high school sweetheart, and a year later, they were blessed with a child. A daughter, they named her Rosa, after Josef's mother, who along with his father had died while Josef was in college. He doted on the child and his wife, buying them every extravagance a teacher could afford. His life was perfect.

But the war changed everything. Josef had been teaching for two years when he was called up for military duty. Tatiana cried endlessly. Reports had been filtering in for some time about the numbers of men who were giving their lives in service of the Führer, and Tatiana was convinced that Josef would never return to them.

He had only three days to report after his notice arrived

and the entire third day, Josef knew, would be spent traveling. The first, he spent in shock with a fussy baby and a hysterical wife. The second morning, his last with his family, Josef dressed in his only suit and took his small family by rail outside Cologne to visit Tatiana's family on their tiny farm. There he talked with Tatiana's father and brother while she took comfort in the presence of her mother. That afternoon, Josef pulled Rosa in an old wagon and briefly posed with Tatiana and the baby for her brother, an amateur photographer, who later sent the small photograph to Josef by mail. Assigned to the Kriegsmarine, Josef labored as a cadet until spotted on duty one day in port by his old friend, Hans Gunther Kuhlmann. Kuhlmann, about to begin sea trials of the newly outfitted U-166, demanded an English translator as part of his crew and pointed to "that man . . . the one with the broom," as an example of one who could fill the position. He had heard the man, Kuhlmann said in what was not quite a lie, teaching English to children.

Bilingual crew members were in great demand, especially aboard U-boats, whose men sometimes found themselves thousands of miles from friendly food and fuel. The Nazi gold each submarine carried for just such a purpose would often be used as payment for these necessities.

Bilingual crews were one thing, but Kuhlmann knew the area of the world to which he was about to be sent. He needed a man absolutely fluent in English. That the man he demanded happened to be his best friend, well, that was a bonus and could remain their little secret.

Josef, for his part, was delighted. He and his boyhood friend shared a common philosophy about the war. That much was established immediately. The two men fought for

Germany and had their own reasons for doing so . . . but both had refused the opportunity to join the Nazi Party.

Once on board, Josef was quickly promoted from cadet to sub, or under, lieutenant, and he became the commander's unofficial right hand during the submarine's sea trials. These exercises, conducted in hostile waters during wartime, were much riskier than a typical shakedown cruise. Therefore, when the U-166 was caught on the surface by a British Spitfire, it was not totally unexpected. The Royal Air Force pilot had strafed them, and scrambling to get off the conning tower where he was stationed with his captain, Josef pushed Kuhlmann down the hatch and away from the hail of bullets. For this act, he was awarded the Iron Cross, Second Class, and at the insistence of Kuhlmann, he wore the ribbon as a part of his uniform. The medal he carried in his pocket, though its very existence embarrassed him greatly. When Josef "saved" the U-166 commander, he was only trying to get out of the way.

Josef saw Tatiana and Rosa only once more after joining the U-166. With a three-day pass—May 28–31—he spent much of the time traveling home to the tiny apartment in Cologne. The hours were precious, but he had been exhausted. Josef slept on the threadbare couch for much of his visit, Rosa climbing all over her father, Tatiana quietly stroking the face of the man she loved.

Had it been only sixteen days? Josef blinked his eyes several times and carefully placed the photograph back into his waterproof submariner's pack. Sixteen days seemed to have lasted a lifetime. Josef stood. Kuhlmann had left him in his cabin, ostensibly to clean, but in reality affording his friend the only luxury there was on a Type IXC—privacy. Josef was grateful and had taken the moment to dream of his family.

As he stepped through Kuhlmann's curtain, the present once again washed over him like a foul tide.

"Landermann!"

Josef turned toward the sound of the voice. It was Ernst Schneider, the boat's official observer. As a Nazi Party representative, Schneider sailed with the U-166 for the purpose of watching and reporting the actions and attitudes of the officers and crew. It was a task deemed especially important in the Unterseebootwaffe. Sub commanders were an independent lot, after all. Thinking "beyond the circumstance" was their stock-in-trade. It was often what kept their crew alive, but this independent thinking, it was feared, could lead to independent action . . . and *that* could never be tolerated.

"Landermann!" the observer called again as he approached.

"Yes?" Josef coolly replied.

Narrowing his eyes, Schneider said, "You will address me as 'sir.'"

Josef crossed his arms and tilted his head. "I am required to address the officers of this boat as 'sir.' You, however, are not an officer of this boat. Therefore, I will address you with respect, but as I please."

Schneider stared hard at him, choosing for the moment to ignore the slight, and said, "I want to meet you and Commander Kuhlmann in the mess immediately. Retrieve him for me, please. I will wait there." He turned to go, then turned back and added, "And don't push me, Landermann. I hold your life in my hands."

Josef watched Schneider move away, confident that what the man said was true. It was rumored that on his last assignment, a gunboat, Schneider's observations had resulted in four men having been shot—one of them an officer.

Josef had no doubt about what Schneider would do if he were goaded, but it simply wasn't in him to roll over for a bully . . . and this one in particular. Hans Kuhlmann wasn't the only man on the U-166 Josef had known when he came aboard. Schneider had also attended Oxford in the same scholarship program of which Josef was a part. The two men were the same age, twenty-six, attended several of the same classes, were fluent in English—but beyond the veneer, they were as different as a puppy and a snake.

Ernst Schneider had grown up on the streets of Berlin. His father, a machinist by trade, was a drunk who beat his wife and daughters but, curiously, never his son. Perhaps that was partly why Ernst arrived at Oxford with a sense of entitlement. He was dark-haired, square-jawed, tall, and strikingly handsome. Students were initially drawn to this physically attractive young man, but soon shied from his arrogant, sometimes cruel, manner. This bearing was on display in the classroom as well as on the athletic field and in social settings.

Among the faculty and students, it was well known that Schneider had joined the Nazi Party as soon as it had been promoted on campus. To be sure, he was not the only one, but he was its most ardent promoter. Ernst Schneider was proud of the newly formed party and openly proclaimed its merits to anyone who would listen.

Josef had been a member of a historical discussion group at Oxford for a time that included the girl whom Schneider dated. She was absent for several sessions, then returned with bruises that had yet to heal on her face. The young woman explained the marks with a story about an automobile accident, but Josef wondered. After all, the discoloration was not only on the front of her face, but on the sides and the back of her neck as well. What kind of automobile accident did that?

Schneider was finally expelled from Oxford at the beginning of his third year. And Josef knew why. After all, he had had a front row seat to the beating Schneider delivered to an art history professor in front of the man's class. It had been savage and swift. The professor had been commenting favorably on the work of Britain's own Jacob Epstein, a sculptor in huge favor at the time with the bohemian crowd, when he also mentioned that Epstein was a Jew.

The class, Josef included, had watched in slack-jawed wonder as Schneider strode to the front of the room and casually picked up a bronze bust from the professor's desk. Then, before anyone knew what was happening or could react, he grabbed the older man's hair and smashed the heavy object into the professor's face. Schneider got in four vicious blows before Josef and another student restrained him. How Schneider had gotten out of the country and avoided arrest Josef never knew.

The two men had been only passing acquaintances at Oxford, and "For God's sake, stop!" had been the only four words Josef had ever spoken to his classmate. But when Josef arrived aboard the U-166 as the boat's new translator, Schneider recognized him immediately.

"We do not need this man," Schneider protested to Commander Kuhlmann. "I can be the boat's translator. I speak English flawlessly."

"That may be so," Kuhlmann responded, "but I speak English only to a moderate degree, and I want to be certain that the exact words I ask to be spoken . . . are the words actually coming from my translator's mouth. Do I make myself clear?" And just like that, before the submarine ever sailed, Ernst Schneider had two enemies on board.

Schneider did not stand as the commander entered the mess with his under-lieutenant. "Gentlemen," he said, "join me."

Kuhlmann never met Schneider's eyes. He went instead to the coffeepot and slowly poured Josef, then himself, a cup. Only after taking a sip of the bitter liquid did he motion for Josef to sit down. The commander offered nothing—coffee or a nod of recognition—to the party's official observer. After another swallow, he finally looked at the man and said, "Yes?"

Not intimidated in the least, Ernst Schneider removed a notepad from his jacket pocket. "Commander Kuhlmann," he began, "I have asked you and your translator to join me as I construct my report on our latest enemy contact." He leaned forward and dramatically poised his pen above the paper. "Could you explain, please, why the crew of the freighter *Gertrude* was warned before the attack, at significant risk to this vessel I might add, then not only allowed to go free, but given our own precious provisions and directions as well?"

Kuhlmann seemed to consider the question. "Because it's my wife's name?" he answered.

Josef snorted, stifling a laugh as Schneider quickly looked from one to the other. "Pardon?"

"Gertrude is my wife's name," Kuhlmann said slowly as if explaining something to a child. "I thought it only fair that we not shoot her too quickly."

The two men stared at each other unblinking until Schneider, at last, slowly leaned back in his chair and closed his notebook. Placing his pen back into his jacket pocket, he said, "I am pleased that you find this a source of amusement, Commander. I assure you, my superiors will not. Look here, you placed this vessel in jeopardy . . ."

"No, you look here," Kuhlmann interrupted. "At no time was the 166 in danger. The target was identified as unarmed and lightly crewed. As for allowing the men to go free, what would you have me do, shoot them in the water? The freighter's crew are noncombatants. The freighter's supplies were the enemy, not the men. And giving two canteens of water and compass bearings was the least a decent human being could do. Certainly I hope the Allies would do our merchant seamen the same courtesy."

"The Fatherland is at war," Schneider growled back. "I am confident the Führer does not desire courteous U-boat commanders."

"Do not forget who is in charge here, *Mr.* Schneider. You are overstepping your bounds. I make the decisions on this boat. Only my judgment determines the methods utilized in the prosecution of a target."

Schneider calmly stood to leave. "Perhaps it is you who are overstepping the bounds, Commander Kuhlmann. Do not forget, I have been briefed on the mission as well. As the official party presence on board the U-166, I am sure that you are aware of my authority to order mission changes according to the coded messages I will be receiving on this voyage. Do not play with me, Commander. You may disregard my bark, but you'll find my bite eminently worse . . . and occasionally final."

As Schneider stalked haughtily from the mess, Kuhlmann's shoulders slumped. Josef, who had not spoken a word during the entire encounter, gave his friend a questioning look. Kuhlmann spoke quietly. "He is right, Josef.

Not morally, of course, but in accordance with the wishes of the High Command. We are to take no prisoners and leave no man to oppose the Fatherland ever again."

"Why don't you do as they demand?" Josef asked, though he knew the answer.

"I must live with myself after the war. My children must be able to look their father in the eye. I fight for my country, Josef, not for the psychopath who has kidnapped her and turned her into a whore."

Though Josef agreed, he quickly glanced around to make sure no one heard the words of his friend. "Don't talk while you are angry, Hans," he said. "Words such as these will surely get you shot."

"But I am always angry, Josef. That is the problem."

To change the subject, Josef asked, "What did Schneider mean when he said he could change our mission? What was that about coded messages?"

Kuhlmann gazed blankly into his coffee cup before answering. When he did so, it was with a suspicious expression. "Again, he is correct, but I do not understand why. Do you remember the day of Hitler's inspection?"

"Of course. It was less than a month ago."

"Why were we herded onto the gunboat across the pier? Why do you inspect a U-boat crew on the deck of a gunboat?"

"You told me it was because of the Führer's security."

"Yes, this is what I was told at first. However, Admiral Doenitz informed me later, personally, that our mission might have an additional aspect. What that addition was, he did not say . . ." Kuhlmann smiled ruefully and peered at his friend from the corners of his eyes. ". . . and naturally I did not ask."

"Naturally," Josef agreed.

"But he did tell me that a special antenna and radio equipment were being added to the U-166 as we stood at attention for Adolf." Again, Josef glanced around. "So that was the real reason we were inspected on the gunboat. It is insanity. They keep secrets about the boat and its mission from the commander of the boat! The admiral also told me that this swine, Schneider, would be receiving the coded messages and would keep *me* informed."

Kuhlmann sighed and stood. Josef stood with him. About to enter the hallway from the mess, Kuhlmann asked quietly, "How are you faring? With . . . you know . . ." He shrugged.

"I've thought about killing myself," Josef responded.

Kuhlmann looked at his friend for a moment without expression. "I don't blame you," he said. "You won't, though, will you?"

"No."

"Good man," Kuhlmann said and nodded as the two men exited the tiny room and walked the narrow passageway, each in a separate direction.

CHAPTER 5

July 18, 1942

IT WAS RAINING HARD. IT WAS ALSO SATURDAY, WHICH meant that it was Helen Mason's morning to open the Hungry Mullet Café. And it was 4:30 AM, which meant that Helen was on time. Helen hated Saturdays. But then, she hated Wednesdays too. And Mondays. And Thursdays and the rest of the week as well. But Saturdays were the worst.

Saturdays meant that Helen had to be up by 3:30 to brush out her hair, put on the smallest possible amount of makeup with which she could still appear to have cared, and slip into the ridiculous white uniform all waitresses south of Virginia seemed to wear. Only then, feeling like a nursing school dropout, would she drive her aunt's old pickup twelve miles on mostly unpaved roads to unlock a coffee shop that no one patronized until at least 6:00.

The ride in this morning had been horrendous. The driver's side windshield wiper was not working, forcing Helen to lean over in order to see out the passenger side. It had been raining for two days, and the road from the cottage to Highway 3 was washed out in several places.

She slammed the heavy door of the Chevy pickup and

ran through the pouring rain to the café's back entrance. When she finally got the key in the lock and the door opened, Helen pulled the string to the storage room light and discovered that the electricity was out. At that point, even in a day that is just beginning, any other person might have considered the situation and laughed. Another might have cried, a few would have cursed, but most would have simply trudged ahead, accepting the abuse that life sometimes seems to pile on. Helen Mason, however, had grown so bitter that she barely noticed. She had come to expect the worst. And this morning, like most mornings, she got it. So she merely entered the café, pulled out a chair, and sat in the dark.

Helen was twenty-five years old, a native of Maryland's eastern shore, and gorgeous when she smiled, which wasn't often anymore. She was tall and slim with full lips and blue eyes. Her blonde hair was silky and curled naturally when it was cut short, as it usually was. She was twenty-two when she met Captain Tyler Mason, twenty-three when they were married, and twenty-four when he was killed.

Captain Mason, an instructor pilot stationed stateside in the Army Air Force, had volunteered to teach a two-week course to a detached wing of the RAF outside London during February 1941. Tyler kissed his bride of four months good-bye for what was supposed to be a brief interlude in their long, happy life together.

The captain arrived safely in Coventry and set about the task of accomplishing his mission. Within twelve days, the entire RAF wing successfully completed the course he taught, and arrangements were made for him to catch a transport back to the States departing a day earlier than he had planned. Before he could board, however, he was killed in a

Luftwaffe bombing raid early that morning. Captain Mason's effects were packed into an army issue, green canvas bag and returned to his widow.

She was inconsolable. Removing her dead husband's few civilian clothes from their closet, Helen stuffed them into the duffel bag. Out of sight, they were also where she could not smell the cologne that lingered in the collars of the shirts, reminding her of the man she had lost, and continuing to fuel her anguish. Helen's heartache became a resentment that she nourished like a baby, feeding it a steady diet of newspaper reports and radio broadcasts about the war in Europe. She hated Britain for involving her husband and America for letting him go, but Helen's loathing rage was reserved for Germany and her soldiers—the monsters who had killed her husband and destroyed her life.

Helen had worked in the army's main recruiting office in Baltimore, but when Tyler was killed, she angrily refused to go back to work. She was alone in the apartment that had so recently been filled with laughter and love and promise. There were no brothers or sisters to comfort her, for Helen was the only child of an unmarried seamstress whose sole liaison with a furniture salesman a quarter century ago had yielded a child, but not the man's name. Helen had been raised by her mother until she was fifteen, when her mother, absent often to begin with, simply left one evening and never returned. Helen, thrust suddenly into adulthood, worked after school and evenings scraping together a meager living, determined not to be evicted from the tenement house her mother had abandoned.

Helen's mother had an aunt who lived on the coast of Alabama. As far as Helen knew, Jean Evans was her only relative. The seventy-year-old woman was a retired schoolteacher, never married, who had worked diligently to maintain ties with her grandniece. As long as she could remember, Helen had received a steady barrage of postcards and letters from Aunt Jean, and she came to treasure the brightly wrapped presents on her birthday and at Christmas.

Aunt Jean had traveled all the way to Baltimore on several occasions after Helen's mother deserted her in order to build a relationship with the only relative *she* had left—the young woman who appeared to be having such a difficult time. On several occasions, Aunt Jean even offered Helen the opportunity to live with her in Alabama, but the independent girl always refused and her aunt never made an issue of it.

On the happiest day of Helen's life, Aunt Jean was at the wedding. She gave the couple three one-hundred-dollar bills as a gift. It was more money than Helen had ever seen. Life, it seemed at the time, had finally turned around for Helen Mason.

Still sitting in the dark, Helen tapped her polished fingernails on the table, wishing absentmindedly that she smoked. *At least,* she mused, *a cigarette would give me something to pass the time.* The rain continued to beat a hard rhythm against the café's windows. *I am bad luck,* she thought as she sat in the dark. *Everything I touch leaks, breaks, leaves, or dies.*

Feeling sorry for her grandniece after Tyler's death, but truly needing help, Aunt Jean asked Helen to move south. The old woman's chronic sore throat was finally diagnosed as something substantially worse, and so, without much thought, but subconsciously grateful to be needed, Helen gathered everything she owned, including Tyler's duffel bag, and boarded the train in Baltimore, bound for Mobile.

Aunt Jean met her at the station in a blue 1937 Chevrolet pickup and asked Helen to drive home, which she did, noting much later that her aunt never drove again. Four months after her niece arrived, the old lady died, taking with her yet another piece of Helen's fragile heart.

In a simple handwritten will, Aunt Jean left Helen everything she owned. This, of course, included not only her cottage and the truck, but in a shocking surprise about which Helen told no one, a cream-colored envelope in the pantry containing twenty-four more one-hundred-dollar bills. On the front of the envelope, in Aunt Jean's handwriting, were the words: "For Helen with love . . ." She had underlined the word *love*, and then, beneath that line, she printed:

To forgive wrongs darker than death or night . . .
To love, and bear; to hope till Hope creates
From its own wreck the thing it contemplates . . .
Good, great and joyous, beautiful and free.
  —Percy Bysshe Shelley from "Prometheus Unbound"

The light over the back door blinked twice, then came on to stay. Helen stood up and moved to switch on the rest. She unlocked the front door at 5:30 and turned around the Open sign in the window. Helen had two pots of coffee brewed hot and strong at 5:45, just in time for Wan Cooper, the lanky deputy sheriff, who entered the café around 5:50, as he did every day but Sunday.

"Morning, Helen," he said as the bells clanged against the opening door.

"Good morning, Wan," she answered without looking up from the cash register where she was counting out change. "Coffee?"

"I'll get it. You just do your deal. Billy in at six-thirty?"

"Um-hmm . . . as always."

Billy Gilbert, along with his wife, Margaret, owned the Hungry Mullet Café, a title most people shortened to the Café or the Mullet. The tiny restaurant boasted eight tables in addition to the six counter stools that faced the kitchen and was the only place to get a hamburger south of Foley. Margaret had taught school with Helen's aunt Jean until both retired—Jean to writing and her cottage, Margaret to the Mullet.

When Aunt Jean died, the Gilberts offered Helen a job. It was a favor to the young woman, prompted by respect for their departed friend and Helen knew it, but still, she appreciated the gesture and, presently somewhat tied to the area as a homeowner, gratefully accepted the position of waitress/cashier/cook. Helen had been employed by Billy and Margaret for almost a year.

She knew the Gilberts needed her too. Billy and Margaret were in their sixties, busy with the café, and though they were not slowing down, both keenly felt the responsibility of their adult son, Danny. Danny was thirty-one years old and had been born with what would one day be known as Down syndrome.

"Hey, Helen," Wan called from his stool at the counter.

Startled, she looked up and realized she was still at the register by the front door. *I can't keep my mind on anything,* she thought disgustedly as she closed the register drawer a little harder than necessary.

"Helen?" Wan tried again.

"What?" she snapped, causing his eyebrows to rise. Immediately Helen shook her head and apologized. "I'm sorry, Wan. I just . . . well, I'm sorry."

"Hey, no problem," Wan said. "I was just gonna ask if you wanted me to cook some eggs and toast . . . or put the grits on . . . I'm not being a smart aleck . . ." He was treading lightly now. "I just thought maybe I could help."

Helen forced herself to smile weakly. "Thanks, Wan. That'd be great. You get some bacon started."

Wan was almost thirty and had never been married. He had been close a time or two, but for one reason or another, he never followed through. He was six feet tall in his socks, which was how they measured him when he took the county exam for deputy. Soon after Helen had started working at the Mullet, Wan became an every-morning customer, a fact that did not go unnoticed by the Gilberts. Margaret had cautioned him about Helen's probable state of mind and intimated that he not be so obvious in his pursuit of the young widow. It was a suggestion Wan tried desperately to keep in mind, but he was smitten. And everyone knew it but Helen.

Before long, the two were seated side by side at the counter, eating the breakfast they had prepared. The rain, still falling in sheets, was obviously keeping the regulars away, and the Gilberts weren't due for another few minutes.

"So ask me a question," Wan said.

"What?"

"Ask me a question," Wan repeated as he took a last bite of bacon. "Ask me anything you want to know about me."

Helen wasn't in the mood, but the deputy was a good guy, and she didn't want to hurt his feelings. "Okaaayyy . . ." She squinted, then said, "Where'd you get your name?"

"Cooper?" he asked innocently.

Helen smirked. "Ahhh, no."

"Oh, you mean Wan. Well, my mama liked Mexican names."

"You're kidding."

"Nope."

"But it's spelled . . ."

"*W* . . . *a* . . . *n* . . . yeah, I know. But she didn't."

"But why didn't someone—your dad . . . anybody—tell her?"

Wan laughed. "You'da had to know my mama."

The back door opened, letting a gust of wind into the café as the Gilberts, led by Danny, hustled in out of the rain. Helen and Wan stood to greet the wet family, placing their empty plates behind the counter in the open window to the kitchen. "Good morning, everybody!" Danny said enthusiastically as he went immediately to Helen, as he did every day, and kissed her hand. "Good morning, beautiful Helen," he said. "Hello, Wan."

"Hey, Danny," both responded. Helen helped Danny off with his jacket as she greeted Billy and Margaret. She had been apprehensive about their son when she'd first started work at the café. Danny was a large man, and Helen had never been exposed to a person with a mental disability. Once, after observing the fearful expression on Helen's face as Danny ran toward her, Margaret took the younger woman aside and explained that while her son was physically an adult, mentally he would always exist as a sweet ten-year-old boy.

From that day forward, Helen accepted Danny as her special friend. While she was bitter about the rest of her life and tended to be unsmiling and short with everyone else, Danny received the best of Helen Mason. Somehow, subconsciously, Helen suspected that Danny was the only person in the world to whom life had been *more* unfair. She and Danny, Helen decided somewhat defiantly, were kindred spirits.

As for Danny, he adored Helen. He held the door for her, carried things for her, and was forever drawing pictures and making things for her as gifts. "Have you made the coffee, Helen?" Danny asked sternly as he hung up his jacket. It was a question he asked her every morning, even when she arrived after the Gilbert family.

"Yes, sir. I have," Helen said. "Who wants some? Billy? Margaret?"

Soon, they were all settled around the counter with steaming cups. Danny made toast for everyone, including Wan, who never missed the opportunity to eat more. He consumed twice as much as anyone Helen had ever met, and yet there wasn't an ounce of fat on his bony frame. "No customers yet, huh?" Billy asked Helen. She shook her head no.

"Me . . . I'm a customer," Wan said as he put a spoonful of plum jelly on a piece of toast.

"Naw," Billy replied, lighting a cigarette with a match, "you're a eatin' machine. You ain't even human. You know, I'm glad the county reimburses you for eatin' here . . . couldn't nobody but the government afford it."

Everyone chuckled as Wan pouted a bit, ignoring them and folding the toast, taking half the piece in one bite.

Billy poured it on. "Yeah, you're acting sad and everything," he said, "but by God, that don't stop you from eatin'. What'sa matter, Wan? Can't get the whole thing in your mouth at once? I swear, twenty fat people died and came back to life as you!"

Wan rolled his eyes with a smile and took another bite.

Billy loved to pick on Wan. He knew the deputy could take the teasing with a grin and secretly considered him a good example for his son. Years before, Billy had been alone in the café's kitchen one afternoon when Danny had come inside crying, distraught over the names some of the other children had called him. Billy's heart had been broken, but he knew that it was a reality with which his family—and his son in particular—would have to learn to live. "Folks pick at you for two reasons," he had told the sobbing child. "First reason is 'cause they like you. Second is that they're testing you. The way you pass the test is to smile. Then when you pass the test, ever'body'll like you because of your smile. And if they don't . . . well, we don't want them as friends anyway, do we?"

Billy Gilbert had lived in south Alabama his entire life. He was a smallish, thin man with a mischievous personality most often betrayed by his twinkling eyes. His hair, what was left of it, was still mostly dark, and one could tell at a glance that in his younger days, Billy had been a handsome man. Quick to laugh, he was magnetic and generous with his encouragement. People just flat-out liked Billy Gilbert. That affection, it was supposed, was why they didn't kill him when he was a young man after he was revealed to have been selling sugar tablets as "comet pills" in 1910.

In the early part of the twentieth century, when Haley's Comet made its trek through the night sky, there was a great deal of suspicion and precious little information about the extraordinary event obviously unfolding in the heavens. Billy, sensing a once-in-a-lifetime opportunity (literally), made Billy Gil's Comet Pills available as protection from the "poisonous gases contained in a comet's tail." The gullible townsfolk of Foley and the surrounding area bought the tiny white tablets by the bottle full, safe at last to venture into their yards at night, free from the deadly effects of the "demon star."

When it became known that Billy Gil's Comet Pills were also available in the grocery store under the name Domino Brand Coffee Sweetener, folks laughed right along with Billy.

He was well aware that any other man might've been jailed for a stunt like that, but pleased to be a part of the joke, and joining the preacher, mayor, and entire sheriff's department as victims, no one in Foley, Alabama, ever even asked for his money back.

Billy and Margaret had been married forty-six years. They were together as man and wife for a decade and a half before Danny was born. It had been the happiest day of their lives until they realized something was wrong with the baby. Retardation, Billy believed at the time, was a fault of the father. He wasn't sure where he had heard that, but he believed it and sank into the depths of a depression only the guilty can reach. Billy blamed himself. Margaret, however, blamed God.

Margaret had been attracted to "that crazy Billy Gilbert" even when they were kids. She grew up just over the Florida line, but saw Billy once a month at church in Perdido when the preacher came through. She was twenty when they were married, older than her husband by a year, though in 1896, both were considered old to be newlyweds.

Margaret was the oldest child in a family with eight children and, expecting a large family of her own, was disappointed and increasingly resentful as her childbearing years slipped by. Finally, after the joy of a perfect pregnancy came the crushing comprehension that their baby—the child they'd begged God for—was mentally retarded.

Margaret was devastated. *So this is the work of God,* she had thought angrily. *The God I asked into my heart as a ten-year-old girl. The One to whom I have prayed and Mama sang and we all gave our money. This is God's reward for faithfulness?* At that moment, Margaret made a conscious decision to turn her back on everything she had been taught—and believed—about a benevolent God, a heavenly Father who watches and loves and cares.

It was years later, but amazingly both Margaret and Billy found their way to a life happier and more fulfilled than before. It had taken an understanding of a principle they had been slow to recognize—a principle they now call "the heart mender."

Margaret, especially, was eager to share the principle with Helen, but the timing had to be right, she knew. Helen's bitterness had created a hard shell around her that kept everyone away . . . along with any encouragement or information others might share. She was not often rude or even impolite; she was cool. Margaret told Billy one evening, "You know, I just about can't tell if that little girl is about to fly into a rage or burst into tears. Most times, she seems on the verge of both."

The couple knew about the tragic death of Helen's husband when she moved into the area to care for her aunt—there are no secrets in small towns. And when the aunt died, too, Margaret insisted that Billy hire her right away. She was young, Margaret argued at the time, had no family, and was being beaten down by life. It was apparent to Billy that Helen reminded his wife of herself and of her own struggles years before. They didn't need anyone, Billy protested, and with the war on, money was already tight enough. But Margaret won that battle as she did most of them, and Helen came to work the next day.

WAN TOOK HIS SECOND PLATE OF THE MORNING TO THE kitchen. Slowly a few customers began to trickle in, shedding their jackets and raincoats. The deputy paused by the stove to thank Billy, then stopped at the counter with Margaret. "Want some coffee to go?" she asked. "It'll keep you warm 'til the sun comes out . . . supposed to rain for a while, you know." Wan nodded and held out his personal cup, but Margaret noticed his eyes were on Helen as she took an order at the front table. The older woman poured the steaming black liquid and said softly, "Give her time, Wan."

"She seems kind of mean sometimes," he said, never moving his gaze from the beautiful waitress.

Margaret chuckled quietly. "Well, that's all of us now and then, don't you expect? And . . . well, you know what's happened. Helen's been through more than most."

The deputy slowly nodded his head, thanked Margaret for the coffee, and left.

CHAPTER 6

July 19, 1942

UP OR DOWN. IT WAS A TRADE-OFF FOR THE MEN OF THE U-166. On the one hand, a sailor might endure the relentless bucking and pounding of the waves on the surface while enjoying the fresh air that came with an open hatch. On the other, he could appreciate the relative calm of undersea navigation, but would most assuredly suffer the headaches caused by the smell of diesel and sewage.

Occasionally, however, the stars aligned. For three days and nights, the best of both worlds had come together, and the U-166 cruised flat, calm seas. The constant supply of clean air and a steady, even, forward motion had allowed the men a much-needed rest. Moving in an uninterrupted line on a north-northwesterly course, the submarine stalked deeper into the warm waters of the Gulf of Mexico. With all of his officers present as they changed the early-morning watch, Kuhlmann finally revealed their mission.

"Gentlemen, gather 'round, please." The commander stood on the forward section of the conning tower as the last colors of sunrise melted away. The boat had not crossed paths with a target of any sort since the sinking of the

Gertrude. This did not disappoint or surprise Kuhlmann, for they were not hugging the coastline or prowling shipping lanes as they might normally have done. The U-166 was headed for a specific destination.

"Fischer . . . Klein . . . Landermann . . ." The commander called each of his officers by name as they circled him closely. The men wanted to hear every word Kuhlmann spoke and knew they would struggle to do so over the chugging of the surface diesels. ". . . Oppel . . . Wille . . . Traun." The Nazi observer, Schneider, was present as well, but Kuhlmann had failed to acknowledge him. The slight was purposeful and afforded the officers a small degree of smug satisfaction. They didn't like or trust the man any more than did their leader.

"You are the finest officers assembled on the greatest, most modern attack vessel that has ever been produced in the history of warfare. Admiral Doenitz, in his wisdom, has seen fit to use us in a way that will bring glory to your families and your homeland. We are taking the fight to the enemy in his own backyard. We will be joining a wolf pack already patrolling the coastline of the northern Gulf of Mexico. There, the U-166 will seek petroleum tankers and merchant freighters bearing east from Texas ports as well as those leaving New Orleans and the Mississippi River. The other U-boats are already experiencing success beyond imagination. The Americans are off-guard and unprepared. Gentlemen . . . Operation Paukenschlag—Drumbeat—has begun."

The officers listened to their commander with excitement. They had seen this part of the world only on maps, and the opportunity to spring upon the enemy in a completely unexpected location was a fighting man's dream come true. Josef, for his part, barely heard the words his commander and friend was speaking. His gaze was fixed on Schneider . . . who stared back at him with a thinly disguised look of contempt. And there was something else too . . . an expression of . . . what? Advantage? Victory? *An odd countenance,* Josef thought, *on a man whose presence is being disregarded. What is he up to?*

Josef wasn't long in finding out. As the men questioned Kuhlmann about navigation of Gulf routes and fuel-to-distance ratios, Ernst Schneider interrupted. "Commander Kuhlmann." They all turned to see him remove a book from the folds of his jacket. Holding it forward, he asked, "What is this?" The first warm rays of the morning sun were just streaking above the horizon, but Josef felt a distinct chill run down his spine.

The book's cover was red hardboard with black lettering. A circular stain from a carelessly placed water glass dirtied the front of the book to the right of its title. Josef recognized the object in Schneider's hand, for it was his. And it had been hidden in Kuhlmann's bunk—a location both Josef and Hans had been certain would be safe from Schneider's prying.

Kuhlmann recognized it too, and figuring the best defense was to attack, he spoke immediately and loudly. "Schneider! I will have you in chains for this! That book is mine and was in my stateroom. You dare to enter my private quarters without my permission? Wille, Fischer, arrest this man and confine him to the engine room."

One look from Schneider was all it took to stop Wille, the chief quartermaster, and Seaman Second Class Fischer in their tracks. Unsure of themselves, they looked to Kuhlmann again, but before he could urge them on, Schneider spoke, not intimidated in the least. "You will not arrest me, Commander, and you know why. Point one . . . I have also been given a mission on this voyage—by the admiral himself—and as I am the only one able to decipher the enigma code pertaining to that mission, you will stand well clear of me.

"In addition, I do *not* believe this book is yours." He cocked his head curiously and held the book loosely in front of him, turning it and bouncing it in his hand. "This book is typeset in English, and forgive me, but I do not judge your command of the language sufficient to digest a tome of this complexity and magnitude." Schneider paused dramatically and affected a casual attitude, flipping through the pages as if he had all the time in the world. No one dared breathe as he held the book aloft again. He turned sharply and pointed the book at Josef. "I believe this book is yours."

The men unconsciously moved away from Josef, leaving him to stand alone, facing his accuser. "And all this time, Landermann, I thought you were cleaning the commander's stateroom . . . a cabin boy . . . now it appears you are a traitor as well." Schneider made a *tsk, tsk* sound as he shook his head.

Schneider held the book up for all to see and read its title aloud in German: "*Im Westen Nichts Neues.*" The men glanced nervously from Schneider to Kuhlmann as the Nazi continued to berate Josef. Moving closer, he said, "You are aware—everyone is aware—that this book is illegal?" Josef did not speak. "Come now, Landermann . . . did you not remember that I can read English as well as you? Did you think I would not recognize Remarque's classic? But help me here, Landermann . . . if every copy of *All Quiet on the Western Front* has been burned by specific order of the Führer . . . what is an English translation of it doing in your possession?" Schneider shifted his eyes toward Kuhlmann. "And in *your* stateroom?"

The observer let the thought hang in the air for a moment, then stepped to Josef and extended his hand, palm up. "Sub pack, Landermann," he demanded.

Josef licked his lips and shot his eyes to Hans Kuhlmann, who nodded slightly. "Present your submariner's pack now, Landermann!" Schneider said again more forcefully. Josef never removed his gaze from the handsome, arrogant man as he reached behind, into his trouser pocket, and produced the waterproof pack all Kriegsmariners were required to carry.

The package usually held formal enlistment documents of several types and chained metal identification tags that U-boat crews were required to carry but forbidden to wear. The tags were prohibited because the loose chain could become snagged by running machinery in the tight quarters of a submarine. Not that anyone cared about the danger to the man being snatched off his feet and pulled into a messy death; the concern was about the harm that loose metal might cause one of the Führer's engines.

Schneider snatched the sub pack from Josef and unzipped its waterproof seal. Reaching inside it, he paused, then held it up into the sunlight as if to confirm his initial findings. Disbelief washed across the Nazi observer's face as he removed a single picture. "Where are your papers, Landermann? Where are your tags?"

Josef said nothing.

"Where are your required possessions?" Schneider screamed in Josef's face.

"They were lost in battle." It was a lie, and everyone knew it. Josef was a submariner. There was no battleground per se. He had thrown them away.

For the moment, Schneider regained his poise. "You do not carry Kriegsmarine or party identification on your person? One or the other is required. Instead you have only a photograph of . . ." Schneider frowned, actually looking at the picture for the first time. ". . . of you, a woman, and a child in a wagon?" The Nazi was about to casually toss the photograph into the churning water below, but a sudden something—a wildness perhaps—in Josef's eyes stopped him.

Raising his head as if to think for a moment, he held the photo up by a corner and asked, "What is this? To you, I mean."

"It is *my* identification," Josef responded. "That is who *I* am."

Not finished, but wisely judging Josef's state of mind, Schneider placed the photograph back in the sub pack. He took a deep breath as if to close the matter, then narrowed his eyes and said, "I am adding two more quality photographs to your tiny collection."

Opening his own sub pack, Schneider removed the first. It was a picture of Josef. "I have been saving this. I knew a time would come when I would be able to present it to you." It was the photograph of Josef as a cadet. Schneider had obviously rescued it from the trash. All crew pictures were posted in the wardroom and replaced with new ones as the man achieved higher rank. "I will remove the current photograph in the wardroom. It will not be replaced. After all, you have no identification. Therefore, you do not belong on the wardroom wall. You will, however, keep this picture on your person . . . to remind you of your status. You are no longer a mighty under-lieutenant. You are again a cadet."

Schneider turned quickly and pointed his finger at

Kuhlmann, who was about to protest. "Do not say a word, Commander. You know I have the authority. This man has been caught without proper papers and possessing a publication banned by Adolf Hitler himself."

Schneider turned back to Josef, who glowered at him, watching his sub pack still in Schneider's hands. After all, it contained the only picture he owned of Tatiana and Rosa. He stood poised, waiting to fight if it came to that or to dive in after the picture should this maniac toss it overboard.

"And here is another photograph, Landermann. This one also for you to carry at all times . . . a small reminder of the men to whom your life belongs. See here . . ." Josef stared at the snapshot in Schneider's hand. It was a broad display of Hitler's inspection of the U-166 crew several weeks earlier.

"Do you see, Landermann?" The Nazi pushed the photo directly into Josef's face and spoke to him as if he were a child. "There is you on the front row . . . looking so angry with your unloaded rifle. There is the admiral . . ." Schneider pointed to the men as he identified them. "There is your Führer . . . and look, Landermann, look . . . there I am! Do you see me? Not a perfect picture, to be sure. The photographer only captured the image of my striking face as I look over the heads of the other officers, but I am there.

"And do you see who is *not* in the picture?" Josef could not imagine where the man was going with all this and continued to stand unmoving. "Commander Kuhlmann is not in the picture! So place this photograph in your sub pack. Consider it a gift. Don't worry. I was given several. But if I ask to see it, the photograph had better be there. And look at it occasionally, Landermann. It will remind you that Commander Kuhlmann, your protector, is *not* in the picture. But who *is* in the picture? *I* am in the picture. You belong to *me*."

Schneider leaned directly into Josef's face and snarled, "When we return home, if I can arrange to be there when it happens . . . to watch . . . I do believe I am going to have you shot."

Schneider moved to exit the conning tower, but remembering a slight he had not addressed, he wheeled around to Kuhlmann. With a serpent's smile, he said, "As for having me in chains? You will be fortunate if I do not arrange for *your* execution as well. So, Commander, do not threaten me."

The rain was beginning to ease, but the wind was picking up. Wan was driving the beach road when the call came over the radio. "Go, Doris."

"What's your twenty, Wan?" the dispatcher asked.

"Beach road. Mile marker four."

"Okay, you're it. Some summer folks just came in. They're staying down at the Ramsey house on the peninsula. That's mile marker . . . ahhh . . ."

"Marker nine," Wan interrupted. "I know where it is. What's up?"

"They said cargo boxes and vegetables and stuff started washing up about eight this morning. The house is way back in the dunes, but from the porch, they could see everything coming in. It was raining really hard, you know?"

Wan rolled his eyes. "Yeah, Doris. I know. What else?"

"Well, they went out to the beach—said the surf was real bad—anyway, there's bodies mixed in with the stuff."

"Oh, no."

"Yeah, they didn't know how many, but there was a lot of bananas too."

"A lot of what?"

"Bananas. Tons of bananas all over the place. That's how the people saw the stuff washing ashore from way back in the dunes in the first place. Bananas are yellow, you know?"

"Yeah, Doris. I know. Anything else? I'm headed that way now."

"No, nothing else. I'll call the med crews—bodies and all—so they'll be right behind you. Hey, Wan, did you know bananas would float? I didn't."

Wan pulled into the Ramsey driveway, which was really just another sandy road—almost a half mile long. The Ramseys, he knew, lived in Birmingham and rarely used the place. It was loaned occasionally to friends and was one of eleven cottages in the dunes along a twenty-one-mile stretch of beach that Wan kept an eye on. At least once a month, Wan drove down each of the long driveways. At every location, he dutifully got out, walked around, and went up onto the decks of the small houses built on pilings, checking windows and doors.

Only four of the eleven cottages were permanently occupied—one of which was the place Helen now owned—and none of them was directly on the beach. People who had built close to the beach in the past found out pretty quickly that there was no such thing as "hurricane proof" or "hurricane resistant" or "storm certified" or anything of the kind. When 140-mile-per-hour winds blew a fifteen-foot wall of water over your house . . . well, you could only hope for dry matches and enough wood to build a campfire with what was left.

Parking beside the cottage, the deputy could indeed see the bananas on the beach as he stepped from the vehicle. Walking the three hundred or so yards to the water's edge, Wan saw dark shapes dotted here and there amid the sea of yellow. Crates, most of them were, but as he got closer, he saw bodies too.

There weren't many. Wan could count seven dead men from the beach, but it was a horrifying sight. They had been in the water for a while—fish and crabs had taken their share. Wan waited for the med crew to arrive from Foley and moved upwind, seeking to avoid the foul odor of rotten bananas and decomposing flesh. The rain had stopped, but the southeast wind had built the waves along the shore into big rollers that fluttered the bodies in the water like a house-wife shook out a rug.

It took the med crew over an hour to make it from Foley, but the five men immediately waded into the surf after what they referred to as "the floaters." Wan sat and watched as they performed their gruesome task, and soon, the bodies they recovered—there turned out to be eight—were lined up on the beach. The med crew boss, a large man everyone called "Pal," came over to talk with Wan while the others went to the truck for canvas body bags and stretchers.

"Eight."

"I see," Wan responded simply. What more was there to say? The two stood for a moment, uncomfortable in the presence of what used to be living, breathing people—men who appeared to have been their own age.

Pal cursed and mentioned an invasive procedure he'd like to try on any German he could get his hands on. Wan smiled grimly, then nodding his head to the southwest, said, "Look at this."

Pal cupped his hands over his eyes to shield the glare. As he spotted the object Wan had indicated, the big man's face reddened. He scowled and ran a string of curses out of his mouth in as full a voice as he could muster. "This ain't right, Wan! You know something's up. That dang old man is always showing up at these places." Wan agreed, but both men simply stood on the beach with their hands on their hips and watched. Aside from the occasional curse words— nouns mostly—that Pal threw out over the water, it was all they could really do.

Harris Kramer, his thick gray beard blowing in the wind, steered his boat right into the floating wreckage and began pulling cargo boxes aboard. Kramer ran an oyster house on the south side of Mobile Bay, but by boat, it was a quick trip into the Gulf anytime he desired. A fast run west, then due south around the tip of the peninsula at Fort Morgan took less than thirty minutes. And here he was again at the site of another U-boat attack.

The attacks had taken everyone along the coast by surprise. The submarines had even begun sinking fishing boats, and from Galveston to Tampa Bay, most people were in stunned disbelief. Was this really happening? After all, there was nothing in the newspapers. Or on the radio. But it was real enough. The bodies and wreckage washing up somewhere every day or so were proof of that. Wan and Pal had worked four such sites already this summer, and every time, old Harris Kramer was the first man salvaging the scene.

Salvaging wasn't illegal, so there was truly nothing anyone could do to stop Kramer, but the man was without conscience—Wan thought he was a ghoul. In most towns along the coast, folks would get together to clear the beach and give the food and supplies to the needy. In many cases, they found a way to return the goods to the war effort. But not here. Most of the stuff was snatched up by Harris Kramer and his nasty boat before anyone else got to it.

Most folks heard the boat before they saw it. Named the *Melany,* it was an ugly, fat boat—a converted oyster barge—with a wide back end and a painted red top. Its sound was distinctive, a throbbing gurgle that coughed, spewing raw fuel out its exhaust and into the water.

Pal waded along in the surf, trying to keep pace with the boat, shouting and throwing pieces of wood at the man, but Kramer ignored him and continued to pull in any of the non-perishable items he found with a gaff and stack them on deck. Wan sat and watched this circus as Pal's men arrived and joined their boss, yelling and cursing in the water. *They're wet anyway*, Wan thought, *and everybody hates the old man, so why not?*

There was more reason to hate Harris Kramer than they knew. He had been given a dishonorable discharge from the army during World War I. Caught stealing from the men in his platoon, Kramer wasn't just kicked out—those were different times—he was beaten and humiliated.

Kramer had it in for everyone after that and vowed he would get even with all of them . . . the government especially. Through a friend of a friend, Harris Kramer met an influential German sympathizer and was recruited to sell food and fuel to German U-boats in the Gulf.

It was easy enough, he reasoned—easier than fishing anyway—and the money was good. He had a fuel ration exemption because his seafood business was designated a "necessary provider of food." The Germans usually paid with gold, though once he was compensated in U.S. currency.

There was no chance of getting caught that he could

determine. The transactions were handled at night, but even if they had taken place in the light of day, who was going to see anything? Everyone was so scared of the U-boats, most times Kramer was out on the water alone. And the kicker? Harris Kramer knew the areas being patrolled by the U-boats—after all, he fueled them—so it was a simple matter of cruising the beaches every day till he found a cargo to salvage. Then he sold to the Germans the food he had gathered from the torpedoed ships. It was beautiful!

Finally Pal and his men wandered back to where Wan was still sitting. Kramer, they decided, couldn't hear them anyway. He was cruising deeper water, searching for anything that he'd missed, and was headed back to the west from whence he'd come.

Pal plopped down in the sand next to Wan just as the sun came out for the first time that day. "Better hustle them dead fellers over the dunes pretty quick. Gonna be hot soon. Don't want to deal with that." Wan grunted in agreement. "What do you think about this U-boat mess, Wan? What're they gonna do?"

"By 'they,'" Wan asked, "you mean the navy?"

Pal shrugged. "Navy . . . Coast Guard . . . Women's Auxiliary at the Baptist church . . . hey, man, somebody better *do* something!"

The men got to their feet. "I don't know that anybody knows what *to* do, Pal. You can't see 'em . . . can't hear 'em . . . it's a whole new style of fighting a war."

"It is that," the big man agreed. "It sure is that."

But it wasn't, really. At least the submarine itself wasn't a new weapon. In fact, the idea of undersea stealth was almost as old as recorded history. In 413 BC, warriors trained in the art of "breath holding" were employed at the siege of Syracuse. They swam undetected for long distances in order to disable ships of war. During the Middle Ages, while the Crusaders surrounded Acre, written accounts confirm an "underwater device" used by the Arabs to gain entry.

Even Leonardo da Vinci drew blueprints for some sort of underwater transport. His design was not seen until after his death, however, and his sketch notes revealed his apprehension that such a device might be used to sink ships.

During the next several centuries, inventors created increasingly sophisticated submersibles. No less a wartime expert than George Washington personally witnessed the launch of a one-man, pedal-powered submarine into New York harbor on September 6, 1776. Despite its ultimate failure as an attack vessel, Washington called it "an effort of genius."

It wasn't until 1864, during America's Civil War, that the CSS *Hunley* became the first submarine effectively used as an offensive weapon. On a chilly February night, the Confederate sub eased out of Charleston harbor and sank the USS *Housatonic*—a brand-new twelve-hundred-ton Union frigate. The explosives had been attached to a long pole protruding from the submarine's bow, and they were detonated by ramming its target. The obvious success of the *Hunley*'s mission was tempered by the fact that the subsequent explosion also sank her, killing all eight men aboard.

The evolution of underwater warfare had been achingly slow, but in July 1942, along the northern coast of the Gulf of Mexico, the German U-boat had reached an unimaginable level of effectiveness. And as Deputy Wan Cooper watched the med crew load the last of the bodies into their truck, he wiped his forehead with a white handkerchief, blithely unaware that, in his wildest dreams, he couldn't have conjured up a story as unlikely as the one in which he was about to become involved.

CHAPTER 7

WHEN ERNST SCHNEIDER DEPARTED THE CONNING TOWER,
Kuhlmann rolled his eyes dramatically for the benefit of his
men, who were already muttering ominously among themselves. Josef was a popular man aboard, as was their commander, and to say the officers did not appreciate the manner
in which the sinister Nazi observer had just threatened their
friends would be to understate their anger.

Particularly incensed was Chief Quartermaster Friedrich
Wille, who, at thirty, was the only man on board the U-166
older than Kuhlmann. Wille was also terribly embarrassed
that he had not arrested Schneider immediately when he had
been ordered to do so. As Fischer assumed the forward lookout and the other officers, their watch concluded, descended
the tower ladder into the boat, Wille approached Kuhlmann
and Josef.

The two men still stood at the back of the conning
tower's Wintergarten, the widely railed open area surrounding the twenty-millimeter antiaircraft gun. They made room
for the quartermaster to join them. "Chief?" Kuhlmann said
as he came near.

Wille stopped and looked at his feet. "Commander . . . I
should be disciplined . . . There is no excuse for what I . . ."

Kuhlmann waved off the apology. "Wille, you are a good man. Good men are often at a loss for the proper way to handle an evil snake when it slithers into their midst."

Emboldened, the chief glanced over his shoulder to assure himself of Fischer's location, then spoke quietly. "Sir . . . there are many forms an accident can take on a boat of this type. We are far from home and . . ."

Kuhlmann held up a hand to stop the man from saying any more. "Chief, don't consider it. I appreciate the sentiment, certainly, but in the middle of all this craziness, we cannot become like them." He clapped the man on the back. "Take your watch, Wille. Go forward with Fischer for the time being. Landermann and I will remain on this station for a bit."

Josef watched the quartermaster move away. He was aware of the freshening breeze in his face as he looked to the south, his eyes drawn to the schools of yellowfin tuna blasting baitfish as they tumbled in the submarine's violent wake. In truth, he had thought about killing Schneider as well. *Wille is correct,* Josef mused, *there are many ways for a man to die at sea. A loose shirt jerked into the revolving pistons . . . a gentle push at night from the tower deck . . . even a pillow over a man's face could accomplish the deed. After all, who would know? Who would care?*

As Schneider had humiliated him in front of the other men moments ago, Josef had actually thought that he might grab the man and simply go overboard, taking him down and drowning them both. After all, Schneider would be no great loss to anyone, and as for himself . . . well, wasn't he intending to commit suicide anyway? Wasn't that why he had torn up his documents on his last watch, tossing the pieces one at a time into the dark waters below? Why hadn't he done it?

Wasn't that what they called "killing two birds with one stone"?

"Josef?" Alone for the moment, Hans intruded on his friend's dark fantasy. "Are you all right?" Josef didn't answer. "Do not worry, Josef. I will take care of Schneider when we return. He will not have anyone shot."

Josef managed an unconvincing nod. "He has done it before," he said. "And he was a psychopath long before he had any authority from the other psychopaths. Remember, I knew him in England."

"I remember. He was like this even then?"

Josef ignored the question. "I am concerned only for you. Maybe Wille has the right idea. *You* called Schneider a snake slithering into our midst. What do you do with a snake? You cut his head off so that he may never bite again." Hans made no reply, and for a time, the men stood quietly, scanning the horizon with their eyes, but searching their hearts with their thoughts.

The U-166 moved at a brisk pace. Capable of speeds in excess of eighteen knots, her beam of 22 feet combined with a length of 252 feet created a draft greater than if a house had been towed through the water. The Type IXC was a long-range workhorse, but she was complex and, in order to function properly, required the efforts of every one of her fifty-two crew members.

As the sun grew higher in the sky, Josef noticed that his friend, the commander of the boat, had not departed the conning tower. *A silent show of support,* he realized. *And much appreciated.* "Hans?" Josef spoke aloud. "What is our location?"

"When I ran the figures at dawn, we were approximately 260 nautical miles from the Mississippi Sound . . . south of

New Orleans. We are to be part of an array of five U-boats shutting the port down and sinking anything in or out. Our last message ordered us in line, nearest the coast, on the eastern edge of the channel."

"Two hundred sixty miles . . ." Josef did the math in his head. "At this speed, we should be nearing the coast in twelve to thirteen hours . . . tonight."

Kuhlmann nodded. "Assuming the weather doesn't change, the south wind will create a following sea for the remainder of the voyage."

Josef and Hans shifted in response to a noise behind them. Helmut Stenzel, the radio operator, stood at attention, having just loudly cleared his throat. The officers had not heard him climb the ladder. He was a young man, thin and pale. Hans didn't ever remember seeing the cadet topside except for an inspection or a forced swim—the submariner's version of a bath. His mental image of the boy—to Hans, he *was* a boy—was one of a stick figure folded behind a tiny desk, his eyes covered with his hands, summoning every particle of concentration into the massive headphones he wore.

"Stenzel?" the commander said in a questioning tone. "What are you doing away from your post?"

"Well, sir . . . ," he stammered. "I . . . ahhhh . . . I have been away from my station for some time, sir. I felt you should be informed."

Kuhlmann frowned, an expression of confusion evident on his face. "What? *Why* have you been away from your station?"

Stenzel glanced around and stepped forward nervously. "Because Mr. Schneider is using the radio, sir. He is transmitting and receiving code through the enigma discs, sir . . . for more than twenty minutes now. I felt you should know."

Kuhlmann dismissed the cadet and looked in Josef's eyes. Josef saw concern on his friend's face. The enigma codes were, supposedly, unbreakable, and if Schneider had been given his own set—as he had asserted—then there was no way to find out what was being transmitted—or received—until the Nazi was ready to tell them.

This could not be good.

MARGARET SCRAPED THE GRIDDLE WITH A SPATULA BLADE AND watched Helen through the kitchen's open window as the young woman cleared the last of the tables from the lunchtime crowd. *Actually it wasn't much of a crowd today,* Margaret thought. Among others, Wan had not come in, which was unusual. Neither had the med crew guys from the hospital. Margaret's imagination quickly spun through the awful possibilities and dismissed any personal concern. In the past, when that particular group was absent, it meant an accident of some kind, but her family, she concluded, was safe. Billy and Danny had just walked out the door, on their way to Mobile for supplies, so it couldn't have been them.

Helen backed through the swinging door into the kitchen, a tray of dirty dishes in her hands, and set the whole lot beside the huge sink. "I'll go ahead and wash these if it's okay," Helen said. "There's no one left out front."

"Fine, thanks," Margaret responded. "I can keep an eye out from here . . . or at least we'll hear those elephant bells if someone comes in."

Helen grinned. The bells on the café door were the source of a running feud between Billy and Margaret. "Just because you're deaf as a post," Margaret would say, "doesn't mean the rest of us want to hear bells that belong in a church steeple pounding the front door all day long."

Billy *was* somewhat hard of hearing, but the slight disability only manifested itself when he didn't want to hear what was being said. And so, as far as his wife's complaining about the bells on the café's door, she was correct—he was deaf. Harder to ignore, however, were the people who knew about the disagreement, were amused by it, and purposefully banged the bells against the door several times as they entered just to get Billy and Margaret going again.

As Helen ran the sink full of hot water, she listened to Margaret hum an unrecognizable tune, still leaning into the spatula, cleaning the griddle. It took anyone assigned to that task much longer than it normally would have to complete. Steel wool was virtually unavailable—steel being one of the many items requisitioned for the defense industry.

Even Billy's cigarettes, Lucky Strike, now came in a white-and-red box. They looked strange, having been packaged in green for as long as anyone could remember. But the military needed the green pigments for dyes and paints, and everyone contributed what he could. It was certainly patriotic—even marketable—as the American Tobacco Company found out the following year when it unveiled its radio advertisement: "Lucky Strike Green Has Gone to War!" Sales spiked 38 percent in the following six weeks.

"What time will Danny and Billy be back?" Helen asked.

"Probably about three," Margaret answered. "When we're through in the kitchen, you can go if you need to. We're not exactly overrun with folks screaming for service, so I can hold down the fort 'til then."

"No, that's okay," Helen said without turning around. "No reason to go home. Nobody there waiting on me."

Margaret straightened up and carefully laid the spatula to the side. Helen's comment was typical of the course steered by most conversations with the young woman. Margaret wiped her hands on her apron and stepped to the sink. She said kindly, "Helen, can I ask you something?"

Helen scrubbed hard at an area of dried egg yolk on a plate. "Yes, ma'am."

"Are you mad about something? I mean, I *know* there's a sadness there, but are you mad . . . angry?"

Helen put down the plate and blinked. She hadn't really thought about it in that way, but answered honestly: "Um-hmm. Yes, ma'am."

"Are you angry with anyone in particular?"

Helen thought before she responded. When she did, it wasn't what Margaret expected. "Yes, ma'am, I am. And no offense, but before you ask me who I'm mad at, I'll just tell you the truth. I'm mad at everybody. And if you asked me, 'What about?' I'd say, 'About everything.' I don't want to be. I don't think I always have been. But I am just mad. All the time."

Margaret opened her mouth to reply, but Helen kept talking: "Margaret, I don't want you to think that I'm ungrateful. I appreciate so much what you have done for me. I love you all, but there's something wrong with me. I wake up angry. I dream wild, furious dreams. I don't mean to be, but I'm mad at you for having Billy. I'm mad at Billy for having you. I'm mad at Danny because he's so happy . . ." Without warning, Helen's lip began to quiver, and big tears rolled down her face. "I'm sorry," she said in a trembling voice before, at last, she broke down and wept bitterly.

As Margaret replayed the incident later in her mind, she recalled how the young woman had folded her arms tightly as she cried, holding herself, instead of reaching out to her friend who was present, as another person might have done. "The poor child," she told Billy that night. "She feels alone in a way I can't quite understand. I just stood there and rubbed her back. I didn't think she was ever going to stop crying. When she finally did, we talked a bit—I don't think I helped—then she said she was sorry again for about the twentieth time and left. Lord, I wish there was a phone out at that cottage. I hope she's all right."

AT MIDAFTERNOON, THE U-166 WAS MAKING A COURSE CHANGE. Hans Kuhlmann had followed his young radio operator down into the boat to find Schneider signing off and standing to relinquish the desk. "For you, Commander," the smug Nazi had said as he handed over a single slip of paper.

On it, Kuhlmann saw, Schneider had written a time and a specific longitudinal location. Also, in large script at the top of the page, the High Command code for this alteration preceded the message. This confirmed the authenticity of the instructions, however wary Kuhlmann might have been about receiving orders from Schneider. After all, this new location, with no further directive on what to do once there, appeared to be at least one hundred miles away from the previous orders of destination.

After calculations were made, the submarine, still running on the surface, executed a gradual turn to the right in an easterly direction. Now on a course of 28 degrees, the U-166 would arrive at her intended destination two hours after dark. Kuhlmann would run the last forty miles underwater at a decidedly slower rate of speed. This, he determined, would allow the boat to avoid detection on the surface by the increased air and sea activity of a coastal population. Why, in God's name, he was to surface his boat in a precise location less than two miles off the Alabama coast, Kuhlmann hadn't a clue. But orders were orders—despite the commander's escalating sense of indignation at being forced to accept those orders from a man who was technically a civilian.

When Kuhlmann asked what the U-166 was to accomplish in the surfaced location, Schneider replied, "I will give you that direction when the time comes. The orders are fully authenticated by the High Command so, for the moment, do as you are told. You know as much as you need to know." *It is a good thing,* Hans thought upon reflection, *that the arrogant Nazi moved away immediately after speaking to me in that manner.* He was already beginning to rethink Chief Quartermaster Wille's suggestion.

Josef was still on watch in the Wintergarten and noticed the course change at once. Holding the rear lookout, he saw the wake trail created by the sub's massive diesels bending behind them and was alarmed at first. Was this a mistake? Had an accident occurred on the bridge? A problem with the rudders? But as the U-166 straightened her line and steadied on it, Josef was convinced that their course was intentional. That realization did not lessen his confusion, however.

As the miles droned by, Josef unconsciously created a pattern of search with his eyes. Wake trail, then scan to the horizon's right for 100 degrees . . . back to the wake trail . . . scan to the horizon's left for 100 degrees. Now survey the sky in the same manner. He knew better than to relax this close to America's coast. An airplane, navy destroyer, or

Coast Guard cutter—not to mention a merchant target— might appear at any time. It was well known that victory and defeat, survival and death, were, in most cases, determined by who saw the enemy first.

Surely the Americans are not so unsuspecting as we have been led to believe, Josef thought. *Are they so naïve as to presume that war is fought only in other parts of the world? Certainly not! After all, their newspapers must be full of the sinkings by now.*

Josef shielded his eyes from the sun and studied the strange creature that had taken up station high above him. He had never seen a frigate bird until this trip. One or two of the huge predatory waterfowl seemed always to escort the vessel. Josef marveled at the bird's wingspan—more than eight feet, Hans had told him—and its ability to ride the air currents for hours without flapping its wings. The frigate bird looked like an angel to Josef, giving the impression of calm, motionless flight, without effort, above everything, always watching.

With his back to the conning tower hatch, and knowing himself to be shielded from anyone ascending the stairs, Josef slipped his sub pack from his pocket. Opening it carefully, he ignored the two new additions and removed the photograph of Tatiana and Rosa. He studied the image and smiled at the memory of that day, of Rosa and the wagon. She had been thrilled as he pulled her for almost an hour, bumping endlessly up and down over the tree roots that protruded from the bare ground in the farmhouse's front yard. Josef had placed the child inside the wagon without any thought to the beautiful white day gown his wife had just made for their baby. The wagon, naturally, was filthy, and Tatiana had fussed at Josef for being *oblivious.* That was the word she used before crying, upset that she'd been cross with him on their last day together.

Josef blinked back tears as, with shaking hands, he tenderly slid the small photograph back into the sub pack. He looked up at the frigate bird again. Oh, God, how he missed Tatiana and Rosa. If he could only be with them now. He longed to feel his wife's tender kisses, to watch her sleep, to hear her soft breathing next to him in the dark. In Josef's mind, the sea breeze carried the scent of his child's skin. He closed his eyes and could feel Rosa exploring his face with her tiny fingers. He had not known this capacity for love had existed in him . . . this love that carried with it so much pain.

For the rest of the afternoon, Josef's mind wandered as his eyes, for the most part, remained true to his duty. Beyond the frigate bird and several curious dolphins who rode in the warship's wake for a time, Josef Bartels Landermann, recently demoted Kriegsmarine cadet, saw nothing.

Earlier than he'd expected, Josef was ordered from the tower. Not for a watch change, but to ready the submarine for diving. Within minutes, all crew had assumed station, the ballast was blown, and the monstrous technological wonder began a smooth, steady descent.

Leveling off at one hundred feet, the U-166 continued her course. A bit slower underwater at only eleven knots, she nonetheless ran quietly and efficiently, now on battery power alone. "Since you won't tell me the *purpose* of this departure from our original mission," Kuhlmann said to Schneider on the bridge, "might it be wise to inform me of the situation we can expect? Do you prefer a defensive posture? Should the deck guns be manned? Party hats and whistles? What?"

Schneider continued to gaze coolly around the control area, totally in control of himself, watching the men go about their work as he presented a studied expression of superiority and boredom. Fully aware that he was driving Kuhlmann to distraction, Schneider responded, "Do not attempt to provoke me with sarcasm, Commander, for you do not possess the wit nor I the patience.

"As for this evening's preparations . . . nothing out of the ordinary will be required. A simple rendezvous with a friendly vessel. Nothing to be concerned about." Schneider moved to exit the area, then turning as if he had just remembered something else, smiled and added, "You know? I *do* insist upon Landermann's presence, your trusted translator. No one else topside, save you and me, of course . . ." He thought a moment, then confirmed, "Yes. Yes, I think that will suit my purposes nicely. See to it, Commander Kuhlmann."

THE FIRST THING JOSEF NOTICED WHEN THE U-166 SURFACED was an increase in sea height. It wasn't much, but from a dead calm area of the Gulf, they had obviously worked their way underwater to a location buffeted by what Hans had referred to as "a light wind or very strong breeze." Josef retrieved his uniform jacket and buttoned it quickly over his light cotton shirt. Experience had taught him that even a summer night could deliver a chill if one were to spend more than a few minutes on a damp and windy deck.

Josef didn't wait for Schneider or Kuhlmann to scale the ladder. After the hatch was opened by the crew, it was Josef's responsibility as the lowest ranking member of the topside party to "clear the deck" and make sure all was safe for his superior officers to follow.

Looking up as he climbed, Josef saw stars framed in the circular opening high above him. The wind caught the lip of the sub's open hatch, creating a low tone, an eerie, ominous moan that always sent shivers crawling down Josef's back. He understood how the sound was made. It was the same principle as a child blowing across the mouth of a soda bottle, but the first time they'd heard the unearthly noise, Erwin Klein, the senior lieutenant, had grinned and told them, "The devil is holding us in his hand and to his lips. That is the wailing of his fiery breath." Josef had not laughed with everyone else. Neither had he ever been able to shake the image that comment had forged in his mind.

Stepping onto the conning tower deck, Josef examined the area quickly, looked into the darkness, and motioned Kuhlmann and Schneider up. The wind was from the southwest and stronger than any of them had expected—around fifteen knots—though the seas remained less than three feet.

Josef shared "a look" with Hans as they watched Schneider check the time and slowly turn 360 degrees to search the surrounding waters for . . . what? There was nothing they could see. The waxing half of the midsummer moon, combined with the brilliance of the clear night's stars, provided just enough visibility for the men to see that, indeed, nothing was there.

"Commander," Schneider said. "Order the periscope signal light turned on for ten seconds."

Not predisposed to be helpful, Kuhlmann did nothing at first, but soon shrugged and relayed the order down the tower hatch. At once, the portable white light at the sub's highest point, thirty feet above them, pulsed on. For ten seconds, the single light intruded into the darkness, bathing the three men in a harsh glow, then faded as quickly as it had come. "What now, Mr. Schneider?" Kuhlmann demanded. The Nazi did not answer, and disgusted, Hans didn't bother to ask the question again.

Schneider calmly leaned against the railing of the Wintergarten until, after only a short time, he tilted his head to the side, listening. From the submarine's rear came a noise rapidly increasing in volume. Josef recognized the sound as the engine of another vessel, but obviously it was missing badly, gurgling and firing as if about to fail. Josef smelled the boat's leaking fuel almost as soon as it struggled into view.

It was a shabby boat, a bit over fifty feet in length, Josef guessed, as he watched an older, bearded man step from its cockpit. The engine noise abated somewhat as the vessel slipped out of gear and turned to parallel the much larger submarine. The man on board began coiling a rope near the bow as if to make a throw.

"Are we docking him, Schneider?" Kuhlmann barked over the racket of the nearby boat. "What is this? Is he preparing to tie up?"

"Of course, Commander," Schneider replied loudly. "What did you think? Must I spell out every detail for you? Did you bring the gold?"

Kuhlmann was confused. "What?"

"The gold, Commander. The gold! Surely you understand we must pay this man for his service."

Hans Kuhlmann's face contorted in fury. "Schneider, you idiot! The gold is in the safe! How was I to know we needed payment of any kind? You told me nothing!"

Out of character completely, the Nazi shrugged sheepishly and confessed, "You are right, of course. I do apologize, however, and would return to the safe if I had the combination. Unfortunately only you, Commander, are authorized to open it. And make certain there is a sufficient amount in the bag. I do not yet know the price of our transaction. Hurry now. Landermann and I will see to tying up this vessel."

Shaking his head in small, quick jerks, Kuhlmann cursed sharply and moved to descend the tower ladder. Schneider allowed the tiniest flicker of a smile to cross his face. As the commander disappeared into the U-166, the Nazi motioned for Josef to follow him down the outer ladder of the Wintergarten and onto the main deck.

Meanwhile, the old man in the boat had gone back into the cockpit and was maneuvering alongside the sub. He threw the engine into reverse to slow its forward movement, creating a screeching whine that set Josef's teeth on edge, but he grudgingly admired the captain's expert seamanship as the boat came to rest right in front of him.

"Catch the lines, Landermann," Schneider ordered as the boat's captain hurried to his bow. When the man threw, Josef expertly grabbed the rope out of the air and ran a hitch around the cleat at his feet. He peered down onto the boat, noticing even in the semidarkness that its top was red.

Josef moved to secure the stern line when Schneider stopped him. "One line is enough." Josef shook his head vigorously in objection. After all, even the rawest seaman was aware that at least two lines were needed to off-load supplies from one ship to another in the open ocean—usually many more. Josef was about to argue when he saw Schneider grin broadly. Schneider's expression seemed so out of place for the situation that Josef halted in confusion and glanced around. Had he missed something?

The old man—the captain of the boat—had retreated into the tiny cockpit and peered out of the window. Josef looked up at the conning tower hatch. Hans still had not appeared.

Then, the Nazi draped an arm around his shoulders and pulled him close. What was this?

"I have always hated you, Landermann," he hissed.

Josef shifted his feet to free himself from Schneider's grasp, but the taller man gripped him even tighter. "Do you remember the afternoon at Oxford when you helped pull me from the Jew professor? You were right to do that . . . for I would have killed him and might have been arrested. Even though I hate you, I owe you my thanks."

Josef wrenched himself free from Schneider's grasp and stepped away. Not frightened, but angry, he looked again toward the tower hatch. Still no Hans. Schneider laughed as Josef looked back at him in bewilderment. "Your friend is not here to help you, Landermann." Josef was truly puzzled. *Help me what?* he thought. *What is this lunatic up to?* Then he found out.

Schneider stepped slowly toward Josef. Maintaining a smile, he spoke in a calm manner, just loud enough to be heard. "You are not fit to wear a uniform, Landermann. You disgrace the Führer and his ideals. You embarrass the brave men who have the courage to preserve the purity of our blood. Let me ask you a question. Are you a Jew?"

Josef retreated a few steps, but didn't answer, unsure about what Schneider intended as he continued to approach. "I said, 'Are you a Jew?'" Schneider stopped beside the cleat where the supply boat was tied. Josef was no more than ten feet away.

"Landermann . . ." Schneider began again with a sigh. "Landermann . . . it is my duty as a representative of the Third Reich, the Fatherland, and my Führer to identify those in opposition to the lofty, yet achievable goals we have before us." Schneider paused and raised his eyebrows dramatically. "Josef Bartels Landermann, I believe you to be one of those in opposition. Are you a Jew?" He paused and cocked his head. "Still no answer? Well, it doesn't really matter . . . because you certainly act like one."

And with those words, Schneider pulled a Walther PPK from the folds of his jacket, extended his arm, and pulled the trigger, shooting Josef, then firing at him twice more as he tumbled from the submarine's deck and into the dark water below.

CHAPTER 8

HELEN'S EYES WERE WIDE OPEN. SHE HAD DISCARDED HER pillow and kicked off the sheets more than an hour ago and now lay on her back, staring at the ceiling. It was a warm night, humid, and would have been more uncomfortable if not for the breeze blowing through the open window. An occasional cloud passed over the face of the moon, creating odd shadows in the cottage's only bedroom.

She was unable to sleep, not an unusual situation, but irritating nonetheless. Helen replayed the afternoon's conversation with Margaret in her mind. She had surprised herself, crying like that. Helen hadn't cried in a long time, having been, she felt, "all cried out." She was numb. Her days were marked only by degrees of anger.

But she had been blindsided by the realization of how much she loved and appreciated Margaret, Billy, and especially Danny. And she was embarrassed—*horrified* was a better word—to hear herself admitting that she was angry with them as well.

Helen looked at the alarm clock. It was almost two o'clock in the morning. Picking the pillow off the floor, she doubled it and placed it behind her head, thinking for a moment she might read, then deciding against it.

She thought about the way Margaret had rubbed her back while she wept and tried to remember if her own mother had ever touched her like that. She wasn't sure. Helen recalled Margaret's question about her anger when she had at last regained her composure. "How long do you intend to stay mad?" she had asked. *What a ridiculous question,* Helen thought as she turned onto her side. *As if I have any say in the matter!*

"It's not good for you," Margaret had said. "Holding on to all that anger . . . it's like taking poison and waiting for everyone else to die. There are no hopeless situations, sweetheart, only people who have grown hopeless about them. You still have choices you can make." Helen had begun sobbing again and told the older woman that so many things had been taken from her that she feared anger was all she had left . . . that and pain. *So why should I give up my anger?* she thought. *Then I am left with nothing but pain.*

Helen rolled onto her stomach and put her face in the pillow. The corners of her mouth turned down as she determined she would not cry again. She had not wanted to offend Margaret as she walked out of the café that afternoon, and she had not reacted, but Helen had been appalled at what the woman had suggested she do. "Forgive," Margaret had said. "It is truly your only hope, honey. To forgive is to set a prisoner free . . . and discover the prisoner was you."

When Helen had not responded, Margaret added, "Take a pencil and some paper. Write down all the things that have happened, all the people who have hurt you—including God if you feel that way—and forgive them."

Helen had nodded and left at that point. She drove home madder than ever, and now here she was in the middle of the night, awake again. Awake and thinking about how crazy it would be to actually write down the things that had gone wrong and who had offended her.

She threw her pillow back onto the floor. *Crazy,* Helen thought. *Crazy and impossible. There's not enough paper in the world.*

WAN HAD NOT SEEN A VEHICLE FOR ALMOST TWO HOURS. HE was parked in the back lot of Snapper's Boat Yard on the corner of Keller Road with a view of Highway 3. It was a quiet night, but Sundays, the one night every week Wan worked, were always quiet. When the radio squawked, it startled him so badly that the deputy almost poured his third cup of coffee all over himself.

"Dangit!" Wan said aloud as he tried to lift himself up from the patrol car seat. The hot liquid was burning a track down the bottom of his pants as he sloshed more coffee on his lap, scrambling to set his thermos down.

Finally he grabbed the radio and keyed the mike. "Cooper."

"Wan?"

"Doris?" Wan frowned. "What're you doing there? Where's Roger?"

"He got sick. I mean sick, sick. He ate a whole bag of dried apricots. Agnes Wilcott pitted them and dried them herself. I could've told him they're just like prunes. Sheriff had me come in. Like I didn't already work all day. I told him I'd do it, and you know I don't mind, but if the county thinks I'm . . ."

"Doris," Wan interrupted. "Doris!"

"What?"

"Is there something going on?"

"What do you mean?"

"You radioed me. You're the dispatcher. Is something going on?"

There was a pause before the woman answered, "No, I was just checking on you."

Wan silently fumed. Doris was almost seventy years old and had worked at the sheriff's office since before the county bought radios. She smoked unfiltered Camels, had a voice like a steam wrench, and was the only dispatcher still working who had hollered instructions out the window to whatever deputy was sleeping under the oak tree behind the jail.

She was also the best friend of Wan's grandmother, which always left him with the distinct feeling that he had better not *ever* "talk back." Everyone knew Doris was a bit of a dingbat, but Foley was a small town, and, well, she was *their* dingbat so they just put up with her and never really gave it much thought. It could occasionally be tough, however, to keep her on subject, a trait that frustrated Wan and the other deputies to the point of cussing, screaming fits—but only in the privacy of the squad car and with the radio turned off.

"What's your twenty?" Doris asked with a hacking cough.

"Snapper's."

"Anything happening?"

"Nope. Pal and them boys get their paperwork filed?"

"Yeah. Filed it with Roger 'fore I came in."

Wan thought a moment, then asked, "Do we know anything yet?"

Doris cackled. "Yeah, we know the sheriff's madder'n he's been since the last one. Roger said he called Pensacola, called Biloxi . . . them navy boys still ain't saying nothing."

"How can they say nothing?" Wan asked. "I can't believe it's not in the paper. None of the sinkings *have* been, and we've had, what, four cargo slicks—all with bodies in 'em—on a thirty-mile stretch of beach in the past four weeks? I mean, I don't get it."

"You by yourself?"

Wan shook his head. Of course, he was by himself. It was the middle of the night in a boatyard. Who did she think would be with him? "Yes, ma'am."

"Well, this is just for you, but Dr. Ferguson's nurse, Elenia, told me something about Jarret Delchamps." Delchamps was the local reporter for the *Mobile Press-Register,* the largest newspaper between New Orleans and Tampa.

"Go on," Wan prompted.

"Elenia said she heard Jarret tell the doctor that his big boss had put the 'quietus' on anything about submarines."

"What?"

"Unh-huh. He said some navy officer had come to Mobile—in person—and talked to the head man at the paper. Told 'im the navy was taking care of it and didn't want to panic folks . . . said it was a matter of national security. Practically ordered the paper not to print anything."

"And they're going along with it?" Wan asked incredulously.

"Seems like," Doris said with a smile in her voice, then coughed loudly, several times, right into the microphone. "You ain't reading about it, are you?"

She has a point, the deputy thought, *though it really doesn't matter whether the newspaper prints anything or not. Everyone knows what is happening. Ain't like a big dang secret,* he mused. *Bodies float up five or ten at a time . . . people just naturally seem to talk.* Wan turned on his flashlight to check his pocket watch. It was 12:15 . . . just past midnight.

HELEN SWUNG HER LEGS OVER THE SIDE OF THE BED AND SAT up. She drank from the glass of water on the night table, straightened her cotton nightgown, and ran her hands through her hair. Feeling with her foot, she located the slacks and work shirt she'd thrown on the floor when she had gotten in bed earlier, and slipped them on.

Standing barefooted, she padded softly through the cottage to the front door and opened it, pausing for a moment to feel the wind in her face. Then, closing only the screen door behind her, Helen went down the cottage steps, with her hands in her pockets, and strode toward the beach.

She carefully picked her way through the dunes, seeking to avoid the occasional cactus or sandspur that grew low to the ground. The sea oats waved toward the young woman, bowing at the insistence of the wind coming off the Gulf. It blew Helen's blonde hair into her face and assaulted her senses with a pungent, heavy salt smell that, in someone else's life, she knew, might be welcome, even pleasurable. To Helen, though, the wind was just one more nemesis, something else to fight, and that was why, when she reached the beach, she turned into the wind, walking west, against the unseen force that always seemed to be pushing against her.

Helen walked the beach when she couldn't sleep, which was almost every night, even making the trek when it rained. She ignored the seashells and pieces of driftwood that others found so fascinating, attempting instead to find exhaustion, hoping to escape in the sleep it occasionally brought into her life.

Even at her most depressed, however, Helen was not totally immune to the beauty around her. She enjoyed watching the raccoons and foxes scamper in the tidal pools and was awed by the patience of the herons and the power of the ospreys as they fished along shore. Once, on a calm evening in early May, Helen had stood for more than an hour and watched a dolphin give birth in the deep, still water near Dixie Bar.

Dixie Bar was an enormous stretch of sand extending more than two miles into the Gulf. Created by the outgoing tides of Mobile Bay as they boiled around the Fort Morgan peninsula, the monstrous sandbar was a peril to shipping, but a fisherman's paradise. Functioning as an immense reef, it attracted sea life to waters marked by a pronounced shore-bound current. West or southwest winds fed that current and knocked the tops off the surf, making it easier for fishermen to reach their quarry as the Gulf swept everything in its grasp toward shore.

The white sand squeaked beneath her bare feet as Helen leaned into the night. For almost an hour, she walked on the boundary of the surf's highest reach, not in the soft sand or in the surf, but on the very edge of both. There was a hint of phosphorous in the water, she saw, giving the white foam of the breaking waves an odd, glowing tinge of blue. She smiled faintly at the beautiful sight. In the summer, Wan had told her, late at night the phosphorous was visible, sometimes dramatically so, more often than anyone knew. In fact, he had said, most people had never even heard of this phenomenon, and fewer were privileged to see it.

Helen slowed her pace for a moment and frowned, squinting at a large shape that lay in the edge of the surf fifteen or so yards in front of her. *A dolphin,* she thought, trying to see through the darkness and smart enough not to rush immediately to the poor creature. If it was dead, that was one thing—she had experienced that twice before—but if the animal was only stranded . . . Helen had heard Billy talk about helping a group of men rescue a stranded dolphin. One of them had suffered a broken arm during the experience.

Helen approached cautiously. She had no desire to be hurt by the wild struggles of a panicked creature with no help nearby. Venturing closer, she saw vague movement, but the animal's effort moved it several inches up onto the beach. The dolphin was going the wrong way . . .

In that split second, Helen saw that the form, now only eight feet from her, was not a dolphin, but a human being . . . a man. She gasped and rushed to him. He was on his stomach with arms outstretched, his face in the sand and pointed away from her. As she fell to her knees beside his stricken form, Helen saw blood. It came from his right shoulder, the one closest to her. More blood was on his right leg.

As Helen reached out to touch him, the man moaned, and she realized that she had no idea what to do. She was at least an hour from the cottage and from there, without a phone, almost another hour to help. He could be dead by the time she returned. Helen's mind raced. Had he been in an accident? Was he one of the sailors from the group Wan had seen earlier that day? No, that wasn't possible. Those men, she had heard, had been in the water for days. This man was still bleeding. He couldn't have been hurt too long ago.

Deciding she had no choice but to move the man, Helen first went around to his other side—the way his face was turned—in order to roll him over. He was conscious.

Though he didn't move his head, the man's eyes blinked wildly, trying to focus as she came into view.

"Hang on," Helen murmured. "You're safe. I'm here to help." The man seemed to be clothed in black, she noted absently, though that was probably just because he was wet. *A suit,* she thought, *or a uniform. Not navy . . . merchant marine?*

"Can you help me?" Helen said loudly into the sailor's face. She was speaking over the roar of the pounding surf. "We need to roll you onto your back."

The man coughed and nodded slightly. Helen saw a comprehending look on his face as she got her left arm under his shoulders. She placed her right hand on the man's hip, pushing and lifting with every ounce of her strength. The man shifted his weight with Helen and grunted with effort or pain as she succeeded in moving him onto his back. Immediately Helen, who was on top of him after the maneuver, felt the man draw easier breaths as he quickly began to inhale and exhale deeply.

Spent, Helen raised herself from the man and fell back into a sitting position in the sand beside him. Her shirt hung soaking wet from her thin frame as she wiped sand from her face with a forearm. "Can you speak to me?" she asked, continuing to watch the sailor's face closely. "What happened?"

"I think so," he rasped. "I am shot."

Helen dusted her hands, then reached to remove some of the sand from the man's face and from around his eyes. "We need to get you some help. I live down the beach three or four miles back that . . ." She stopped suddenly. Helen had gestured over her shoulder and glanced away as she had spoken, but a small . . . something . . . had interrupted her thought. Frowning, she looked back at the man on the sand before her and broadened her gaze.

Something wasn't right. Helen looked at the uniform, its ribbon and buttons. Her eyes narrowed, and hot saliva poured into her mouth. Breathing heavily, she said, "You are not an American sailor."

The man said simply, "My name is Josef."

Nausea threatened to overwhelm her. Helen asked flatly, "Are you German?"

"Yes," Josef confirmed.

In that one word, at the precise second it was uttered, Helen experienced an avalanche of emotions raining down upon her consciousness. There were far too many sensations to categorize, or even recognize, so violently and abruptly did they flood upon her. Rage, caution, suspicion, revulsion, despair, opportunity, frustration, satisfaction, hatred, fear . . .

It was amazing, really, with all the choices available to her in that moment that she would choose opportunity, but to Helen, it was the proper selection. After all, it might never present itself again. Helen balled her right hand into a fist, and with everything she had, she punched Josef in the face. Rewinding, she swung her fist into his wounded shoulder. "You filthy bastard!" she shrieked. "You killed my husband!" And she hit him again and again and again.

Finally physically unable to swing and sobbing uncontrollably, Helen crawled off a few steps and threw up. She fell back into the sand and cried again until there was nothing left. Trying for a moment to think rationally, she looked over at the sailor who'd said his name was . . . ? *Who cares what his name is? What do I do now? Should I kill him? Can I kill him? I don't have a knife or a gun . . . I could get him back into the water and hold his head under, but I don't have the energy.*

Helen decided to turn him in when she got to town the next morning. She looked again at the sailor, who lay with his eyes closed. He certainly wasn't going anywhere, at least not far. Wan would be at the café when she got there. He would take care of this.

Shakily Helen got to her feet and began to move away when the man spoke: "I am so sorry about your husband." Helen wanted to run, but Josef's voice carried over the sound of the waves and held her there. "You can hit me more if you want. I do not have the strength, or I would do it for you. Can you kill me?" Josef began to cry. It was a wretched wailing that rose above the dunes and into the sky. His weeping held no tears, but was filled with anguished cries of hopelessness and shame. "Tatiana!" he screamed. "Tatiana! Rosa! Oh, God! My God!"

Helen watched him without expression. After a time, Josef only sobbed. Looking toward her, he addressed the young woman in a voice louder than was necessary: "What was his name?" Helen simply stared at him. He spoke again: "Your husband . . . what was his name?"

"Tyler Mason," Helen replied. "Why do you care?"

He didn't answer.

Not knowing why, and certainly giving it no thought, Helen walked over to Josef, grabbed him by the collar, and jerked. "Get up," she commanded, and with her unpleasant help, he did.

She draped his arm over her shoulder and said, "Walk."

"To where?"

"My house is this way."

Josef struggled for breath and leaned heavily on the

young woman. He felt her strength as she hauled him through the sand. "Why are you helping me?" he asked.

"Who said I was helping you?" she answered. "Shut up."

IT WAS ALMOST DAWN, 5:15, WHEN THEY REACHED THE COTTAGE. Helen dropped him at the bottom of the small home's only stairs. She was already late for work. "There's medicine in the bathroom and water in the icebox. Get up the steps as best you can," she said to Josef. "Or lie here. I don't really care which."

Helen bathed and was ready to leave in ten minutes. Josef still sat on the ground at the bottom of the steps as she drove off. She had not said a word to him when she passed.

Josef propped himself against one of the cottage's pilings and watched as the young woman drove off. *She is a nurse,* he thought, noticing her white uniform. *She helped me because she had to.* Josef knew that nurses and doctors took some kind of an oath that bound them to care for the sick and injured. He looked up the stairs, a distance that seemed impossible, but that he knew was not. What he had just survived was impossible.

Josef had never lost consciousness. Not when he'd been shot, not when he'd finally made it to shore, or not when he made the long walk with the young woman. He had managed that by keeping his mind occupied trying to deconstruct the puzzle of Ernst Schneider's actions of the night before.

It seemed clear to him now that the Nazi had intended to shoot him all along. That was obviously why he had requested Josef as part of the deck party. It was also why he had "forgotten" the gold and sent Hans Kuhlmann below to retrieve it. Schneider wanted to be alone with Josef on the deck of the U-166. And except for the shabbily bearded man in the red-topped boat, they *were* alone. But what cargo had the small boat brought to the submarine that required only three men—no, two men—to off-load it? It couldn't have been much. The boat left shortly after Josef was shot. And when Hans returned to the deck, how could Schneider possibly have explained Josef's absence? There were too many questions and no answers for any of them.

Josef had been stunned when Schneider drew the pistol and aimed at his chest, but not so stunned that he was unable to move. Twisting sideways at the instant of the first shot, he had avoided being mortally wounded, but the impact of the .32 caliber hollow-point bullet in his right shoulder was enough to drive him off the sub's deck and into the water. Schneider had sent two more shots his way, one of which grazed his thigh before Josef had managed to hide in the shadows between the two vessels.

He had dog-paddled with one arm to the other side of the old boat and, there in the dark, held on to one of the tires tied to its rail. Many smaller boats, Josef knew, used old tires as bumpers and had several on both the port and the starboard. When he had heard the diesels rev, Josef held tight and used the boat's forward motion to take him out of the shadow of the U-166. Thirty yards away, he let go, intending to be far enough out for the sub's searchlight to catch him in its glare. He was certain that Kuhlmann, his captain and friend, would soon be searching for him. But the searchlight was never turned on, and Josef had watched in astonishment as the U-166 silently slipped beneath the waves.

Alone and beginning to feel pain from his wounds, Josef had feared not drowning, but sharks. He had known he was bleeding—how badly he could not tell—but Josef knew sharks could find food in an incredibly short period of time. And when they found it, they were not shy or polite. Josef, with the rest of the crew, had always watched in horrified fascination as the garbage was dumped from their decks. The monsters arrived in packs, and they were never long in showing up. *How many times,* Josef had thought as he struggled against the rising panic, *have I dreaded dying this way?*

He had known the wind direction and current were both in his favor. The tide was rushing into the vast mouth of Mobile Bay, sucking everything with it in that direction. The wind and current where Josef floated, hanging to a timber he had washed against, ran almost parallel to the bay mouth's tidal surge. Josef had remembered a huge sand bar from the submarine's area charts. If he could just reach that, he had known, the wind and water would continue to push him toward the beach.

When Josef's feet had finally touched bottom, he walked the bar, alternately being lifted by the waves and swept with the current, for almost two more miles—all the way to the beach. There, he had dropped, almost dead from swallowed seawater, exhaustion, and loss of blood, but grateful for the absence of sharks.

Crawling to the stairway now, Josef looked up at the cottage and wondered briefly how long he had lay in the surf before the young woman had come along. He pulled himself up into a standing position and swayed dizzily. Sitting back down, Josef rested before taking his time and backing his way up the steps, still sitting, to the door above.

BY THE TIME HELEN ARRIVED, WAN HAD ALREADY OPENED the café and made the coffee. As deputy, he had a key to every place in town anyway and knew that Billy wouldn't mind. Wan accepted Helen's terse, "Morning. I over-slept," as all the conversation he would get, and when the Gilberts arrived soon after, they never knew she had been late.

The morning went by without incident. Helen thought Margaret might be watching her a bit more closely than usual, but after their conversation the day before, Helen didn't blame her.

All the talk by the lunch crowd was about the bodies that had floated up and U-boats and whether anybody intended to fish that weekend. "I'll fish from my backyard," Weaver Sullivan told the other men.

"You don't live on the water, Sully," one of them remarked.

"That's right," he responded, "and I ain't likely to be torpedoed off my porch neither." Everyone chuckled grimly.

"Hey, Wan," one of the men called. "What's that old peckerwood Harris Kramer up to? Pal says he's showing up ever' time there's a sinking. That right?"

Wan nodded, but before he could speak, another chimed in. "He ain't selling fish. Nor oysters neither. You know he ain't, Wan. But he sure seems to have plenty of money . . ."

"Not that he's spending any of it on that old death trap of a boat," Billy interrupted. They all laughed, but the implication was clear.

"Got to catch the man to arrest him," Wan said with a shrug.

"Aw, hellfire, Wan," Hal Briggs said as he slid his chair back from the table and stood up. "Ever'body and God knows that creepy old weasel is helping the krauts. Now I say the sheriff and you or somebody ought to go down there and haul him in! Lock him up!" Several of the other men murmured and nodded in agreement.

A big man, Briggs was the president of First National Bank and a deacon at the Baptist church. People tended to listen when he talked, but Wan had an idea no one enjoyed the sound of Briggs's voice as much as Briggs himself. Wan glanced at Billy behind the counter. Billy didn't think much of Hal Briggs and Wan knew it, but Billy merely crossed his arms and smiled at his young friend.

Briggs spoke once more: "Deputy Cooper? Do I need to ask again? Does the sheriff's department intend to do something about Harris Kramer, or do we have to handle it ourselves?"

Helen was watching from the kitchen. She saw Wan flush with anger, but was impressed when he replied in an even, cool voice. "I've already said," he began, "'got to catch the man to arrest him.' You know, guys, there's that tricky little thing about 'innocent until proven guilty.' So right now, no, I can't do nothing. But you, Mr. Hal . . . you go right ahead. That's a mighty nice offer to help. 'Specially since you got the biggest boat in town. I'm thinking all you guys'd fit on it. Get out there tonight. You can catch that joker red-handed, I'm thinkin'." Wan stood up, pulled the money for what he'd eaten out of his wallet, and slapped it on the table. "Matter a fact, when you catch old Kramer tied up to a U-boat . . . arrest the Germans too. Hellfire yourself, Mr. Hal. Bring 'em all in. It'd be a big help."

As Wan walked out, Billy turned toward the kitchen to keep the banker from seeing the grin on his face. Helen had watched the scene anxiously, well aware that she had still not said anything to anyone about the German sailor who was, presumably, still at her house. Helen had intended to tell Wan about the man as soon as she got to the café that morning, but she hadn't—and didn't know why. And she had come close several times. At one point, Helen had even told the deputy she had something to tell him. He followed her to the kitchen, but she froze. Helen ended up stammering and saying again how much she appreciated Wan not saying anything about her being late.

She got off at two o'clock and drove home, furious with herself for having said nothing. *I should have told Billy,* Helen thought. *I should probably go back and get him now. Or Wan. Or somebody.*

When Helen wheeled the truck into the sandy driveway that led to the cottage, she came close to stopping and going back to town. Instead, she parked the truck farther from the cottage than usual, got out, and retrieved the tire tool from the truck bed. The man was not by the steps where she had left him. He was, she knew, either inside or gone . . . neither of which was good. *I am an idiot,* Helen thought. *Go back to town. Helen Mason, go back to town.*

Stalking carefully to the cottage, Helen quietly climbed the stairs and saw a dark stain on one of the steps. Was that blood? Had it been there before? She wasn't sure. The door was not open. *But he could have closed it, right? I wish I had a gun.* Helen stopped. Now, here was a thought that had not occurred to her. *What about him? Does he have a gun? I didn't see one, but then I wouldn't have, really, isn't that correct? What am I thinking?* She reached out with a trembling left hand and placed it on the doorknob. *Helen, you are smarter than this . . . go back to town. Get Wan and Billy. Do not go in that door.*

But she did.

CHAPTER 9

"DADDY, WHY DOES HELEN ACT MEAN?"

The question from Danny came out of the blue, as so many of them did, and did not surprise Billy at all. His son often used the time they spent in Billy's truck to talk endlessly about whatever came to his mind. At least twice a week, the two of them drove to Mobile or Pensacola for supplies. They rode with the windows down—even in the winter, except on the worst days—so that Billy could smoke and Danny could stick his hand out the window and let his fingers "ride the air."

"So why?" Danny asked again.

Billy flicked a cigarette butt out the window. "Well, let me ask you this. Do you think Helen *is* mean?"

"No, Daddy," Danny said impatiently. "I don't think Helen *is* mean . . . I was saying, 'Why does she *act* mean?'"

"Does she always act mean?"

"No. Helen is nice to me. But sometimes, she is mean to Wan. And I saw her be mean to you one time."

Billy turned left onto Highway 98 and steered with his knees as he lit another cigarette.

"Mobile today, right?" Danny said, recognizing the direction.

"That's right, Buddy Boy," Billy answered. "Mobile today."

"So, Daddy, why does Helen act mean?"

Billy had long ago created a level of patience just for Danny. He loved the boy with all his heart. And he was a boy, really, even though he was bigger than most of the men in town. The doctors had told Billy and Margaret that they would discover special gifts in their son that "normal" people did not have. Through the years, Billy especially had found that the doctors had been right.

For one thing, Danny had a persistence about him that tended to annoy others, but allowed the boy successes in many areas. He simply would not stop trying until he achieved whatever he had set out to do. He would not stop asking until he got an answer that satisfied his question. He was not bothered by failure or the passing of time or the seeming impossibility of a task. Billy had been surprised to discover that he admired his son and was grateful for his presence. There existed a wisdom in his child that was different . . . and that he had not expected to find.

Billy blew a thick cloud of smoke toward the window. "Okay . . . ," he said, "why does Helen act mean? Well . . . you know Helen has had some tough things happen in her life . . ."

"I know."

". . . and because of those tough things, Helen has gotten mad."

"Mad at what?"

"Well, Buddy Boy . . . Helen is mad at everything right now. She is a good person, and you are right . . . she is not really mean. But sometimes when a person is angry, that person can *act* mean. Helen has let her anger consume her. Right now it has *become* her. And anger is about the only way Helen expresses herself. You know, if all you have is a hammer . . . everything pretty much looks like a nail." Billy paused. "And that's why Helen acts mean."

Danny was quiet for a bit, looking out the window. Soon he spoke again: "Mama says that if Helen would forgive some people, then she would not be so sad. You are Helen's boss, Daddy. If you tell her to forgive those people, then she will have to do it, and she won't be sad anymore."

Billy chuckled. "I wish it was that simple, sweet boy." He rubbed his face briskly with his hand. "Now, let me see . . . how to explain this . . . Danny, forgiveness can occur only because we have been given the ability to make choices. We have the choice to forgive or not to forgive . . . and nobody can make us do either one. You understand?"

Danny nodded.

"We begin to forgive by *choosing* to forgive . . . by deciding, not by feeling. Our feelings don't lead us to forgive. Most times, our feelings lead us the other way. That's why a person has to decide to forgive first. Our feelings always follow along behind our decisions."

"Forgive and forget, you mean?"

"Hey, Buddy Boy," Billy said, pointing to a gas station ahead, "you want to stop and get a Coke?"

"No, sir."

"You hungry?"

"No, sir."

Billy sighed. Danny wore him out sometimes. He never had to think or focus as much as he did when he was with Danny. He lit another cigarette and glanced at his son, who was leaning against the opposite door, just looking at him. Billy knew it was just a matter of time before he . . . *Okay, here we go . . .*

"Daddy . . . forgive and forget, you mean?"

"Awright." Billy smiled. "Lemme think here." He thumped his ash down in the floorboard of the truck.

"Mama says not to do that."

"Well, she'll just have to forgive me, okay?"

"It's a choice she'll have to make."

"Right. Danny, be quiet. I'm trying to think." Danny crossed his arms and settled back against the door. "Now, you asked," Billy continued, "did I mean 'forgive and forget'?" Danny nodded. "And the answer is no.

"Forgive and forget is not reality. It's not really possible anyway, which is a good thing, because it is not necessary. Forgiveness does not erase history or excuse what happened. What has happened . . . *has* happened, and nothing can erase the memory of it or its consequences.

"Forgiveness means relinquishment. It is that simple. Danny, do you know what relinquishment means?"

"No, sir."

"It means giving something up. To relinquish something means to give up whatever power it holds over us. If you forgive somebody for something he did to you, that means you choose to never again allow that event to determine how you feel or how you act or even how you treat that person. You may *remember* the wrong, but by choosing to forgive, you have disarmed it. Then it can no longer determine what you think, what you say, or what you do." Billy flipped his cigarette out the window. "You got it?"

Danny nodded. "I do."

HELEN DIDN'T KNOW WHETHER SHE WAS RELIEVED OR SCARED to find the German sailor on the floor in the bathroom. "Hey," she said and prodded him with her foot.

Josef was lying on his back. When he opened his eyes and saw her standing over him with a tire iron, he flinched and said, "You aren't going to hit me with that, are you?"

"Maybe. Get out. I have to use the restroom." Helen noted the bruises on his face—both eyes were black—with an odd mixture of happiness and horror. *Did I do that?*

Josef struggled to rise, but fell back almost immediately. "I'm sorry," he said. "I will do it." He tried again.

Helen reached down and took hold of the front of his shirt and pulled. "You're still wet," she remarked.

Josef was scared and having trouble thinking clearly, but the woman's comment still irritated him. *Of course, I am wet,* he thought. *Where do you think I would get any clothes?*

As Helen helped him out of the bathroom and into the hallway, she inadvertently felt his skin. He was burning up. "Wait here," she said. "Give me a minute, and we'll look at your wounds."

While she was in the bathroom, Helen looked through the cabinet. It contained mostly her aunt Jean's medicines that Helen hadn't touched since the final days of the old lady's life. Other than the usual home remedies, the medicine chest was filled with painkillers and experimental drugs for cancer that obviously hadn't worked. *I suppose I'd better look at him first,* she thought, *before I give him any of this stuff. What if it kills him?* Helen shrugged as she unlocked the bathroom door and answered her own question. *So what if it does?*

"Have you looked at your shoulder at all?" she asked.

Now on the floor in the hallway, Josef shook his head no and said, "I am freezing. May I have a blanket?"

Helen stopped briefly, her mind racing. *This man is*

dangerous. Stop, Helen! Stop right now! Get back in the truck and go for help. Move! "First we need to get you out of the wet clothes. Take them off and I will look at the wounds."

Josef looked aghast.

"What's wrong?" Helen asked.

"I cannot take off my clothes," Josef said. "You . . . are a girl."

Helen smirked. "Hurry up and don't be stupid. I am not a girl. I am a woman and I have seen a man before, so just do what I say. Besides, I hate you, remember?"

As it turned out, Helen had to help him out of the wet clothes. To spare him the embarrassment, she didn't insist Josef take off his boxers until he was beneath the blanket. The bullet hole in his shoulder was matched by an exit wound in his back. Helen supposed that to be a positive—that the bullet was not still in his body—and also noted that no bone was broken. The hole in his back was much larger than the one in the front, and although the bleeding had stopped, in its place a yellowish discharge had begun. It was infected, Helen knew—without a doubt.

She poured a whole bottle of rubbing alcohol over the wound and scrubbed it out with a clean rag. The pain was unbearable, and Josef passed out immediately. To Helen's dismay, he was not even conscious to experience the agony as she treated the leg wound in the same manner.

In any case, the leg was not as bad. The bullet had dug a vertical furrow about four inches long and less than an inch deep. While he was out, Helen found a powder labeled "For Infections" and poured it generously onto both wounds and bandaged them up.

When Josef came to, he was still on the floor in the hallway, the blanket over him. The woman was not there that he could see. "Hello . . . ," he called.

Helen came from the bedroom. "How do you feel?"

"Cold."

"Can you get up?"

"Yes." But he couldn't.

Once again, Helen helped Josef stand. This time, she moved him to the couch in her tiny living room and helped him to wrap up in the blanket. He was still without clothes underneath and, while embarrassed, was cold.

"Do you need another blanket?"

"Do you mind?" Josef asked.

"Yes, I do," she answered, but got another one anyway. "The police will be here soon," she lied as she placed the second blanket over him. *Why did I say that?*

"You are a nurse?" Josef asked.

"What? No. I am a waitress." Josef looked confused. "Oh," Helen understood. "The white uniform . . . Nope, not a nurse."

They stared at each other for a moment. Josef through glassy, feverish eyes, and Helen in her perpetual state of anger and distrust. "Are you from a submarine?" she finally asked.

Josef considered her question. Was there any reason to hide the truth? He didn't think so. Was he still fighting for his country? Fighting? No. Well then, was he still even *for* his country? He wasn't sure . . .

"Hey . . ." Helen snapped her fingers. "I asked you a question. Are you from a submarine?"

What is the harm? Josef decided. "Yes."

"Odd wounds for a submariner," Helen observed. "Don't you guys usually drown? Who shot you?"

Again Josef pondered whether to answer, and he cautiously did so: "A man on my boat."

Helen, who was still standing but had moved across the room, raised her eyebrows. "Really? Some friends you have there."

"He was not my friend," Josef said.

"No kidding." Helen leaned against the wall and watched him for a moment. He seemed to be drifting off . . . or about to. "What is your name?"

He answered slowly, "Josef."

"Your whole name."

Josef tried to concentrate, but was feeling worse by the minute. He didn't want to antagonize the young woman. She had almost beaten him to death on the beach the night before and obviously wasn't any more fond of him now. Still, he was so dizzy . . . *What is it that she wants? I am so cold. What is my name? I am a cadet.*

"What is your whole name?"

Tatiana? Is that you?

"Hey? Are you listening to me?"

"HEY? ARE YOU LISTENING TO ME?"

Startled, Helen looked up with a jerk. "I'm sorry, Wan. What did you say?"

The deputy pushed away from the café counter and stood up, shaking his head. "Never mind." He reached in his pocket for his wallet. "It's almost six. Billy and them'll be here soon. Ain't like you need any company 'til then."

"Wan, please. Don't be mad. I'm really sorry."

He put his money on the counter. "Helen, is something wrong? I mean, no offense—you're never really nice to me—

but the past couple of days . . ." He made a futile gesture with his hands. "I mean . . . I only want to be your friend. Geez."

"I'm sorry," Helen said cautiously. "No, nothing's wrong."

The deputy shook his head sadly. "I'm glad, I guess."

Now Helen was confused. "You guess?"

"Yeah. You know . . . it doesn't make me feel great. Nothing's wrong? So you just treat me badly for no reason?" Wan turned to go, then stopped and turned back. "Look, I don't want to make you feel worse. I'm okay. We're friends. You didn't mean to hurt my feelings, did you?"

"No, Wan. Really I . . ."

"Then we're fine," Wan assured her. "Like I said, we're friends. If you ever do need me . . . to talk or anything . . . well, you know . . ."

Helen watched Wan leave through the back door. Wan was her friend and she would not have hurt him for the world, but he was also an officer of the law. And a smart one at that. Helen was terrified.

It had been two days now since the German sailor—Josef—got so sick. He was still on her couch, burning up with fever, sleeping mostly, but talking too. And crying sometimes and shouting. He opened his eyes, but she knew he never saw her. The man was delirious, and she didn't have any idea what to do.

She couldn't call the doctor. And now, she feared she couldn't tell anyone else, either. Sometime yesterday afternoon, Helen realized that she had waited too long to turn the man in. The questions from authorities, she knew, would now be pointed in her direction. She was hiding an enemy of her country.

The first customers came in a few minutes before the Gilberts, and Helen had already taken care of them. Coffee and toast only. "Where's Wan?" was the second thing out of Billy's mouth after "good morning."

"Come and gone already," Helen answered as she entered the kitchen. "I'm afraid he was somewhat aggravated with me."

Danny and Margaret were curious about her statement, but it was Billy who smiled and asked, "Was Wan aggravated at Helen, the waitress? Or at Helen, his friend?"

Helen appreciated Billy's tactful question and answered it with the first smile she'd managed all morning. "Billy, you know he wasn't put out with 'Helen, the waitress.' She's the best one you've got."

"She's the only one I got," Billy said, and they all laughed. He looked out into the dining area. "Pretty light so far. Those guys settled?"

"Done," Helen replied. "Just refills of coffee now."

"Well then," Billy winked, "why don't you three sit at table one right there and let old Billy make your breakfast. Buddy Boy," he said to Danny, "help these two beautiful ladies get seated."

For almost twenty minutes, Helen tried to participate in the conversation with Margaret and Danny. The breakfast, she told Billy more than once, was wonderful. But the man who lay on her couch at home was never far from her mind. It was strange, she thought. *When I found him, I really wanted him to die. Now, I'm afraid he actually might.*

Helen listened to Danny chatter away while mentally calculating her options. *Okay, let's say he dies . . . I can just hear myself . . . "Wan, you know how you said we were buddies? Well, I have this body I need removed . . .*

no, he wasn't a friend, just one of the Führer's finest I was hiding . . ."

Of course, if he lives, it won't be any better—I'll never be able to have a visitor . . . no way that would work. "Come in. Come in. Would you like something to drink? Just ignore the naked Nazi on the couch . . ."

The café slowly filled and slowly emptied. They worked steadily until 8:45 when Billy motioned for Helen to join him in the kitchen. "Do you want to take off early today?" When she didn't answer immediately, Billy added, "You opened yesterday and today and . . . well, Margaret says you got something on your mind."

Helen nodded. "I am tired . . . so if you're sure you don't mind . . ." She was trying to remain calm, but was actually frantic to get home.

"Yeah, go," Billy said, "and you're not the early bird tomorrow so that'll get your sleep caught up." As an after-thought, he asked, "Do you mind dropping Danny off at the church in Foley? I know it's out of your way, but it'd save me a trip. Today's his volunteer day for working in the garden."

"I'd be happy to, Billy," Helen said. "I enjoy Danny's company. And thanks for the time off." She reached up and kissed Billy on the cheek.

"Hey, now," the old man said with a laugh, "if I'm gonna get kisses for time off, then take the rest of the week."

In the few seconds it took Helen to hang her apron on the hook in the back room and say good-bye to Margaret, she and Danny were out the door.

"Do you know the way to the church?" Danny asked as he got into the truck.

"I sure do." Helen smiled.

"There's two of them, you know."

"I know."

"Two churches."

"Right."

"A big one and another big one."

"Which one do you belong to, Danny?"

"The big one."

"Not the other big one?" Helen teased.

"Nope." Danny grinned. "I go to the big one."

Helen headed north on 3. It would take her only about ten minutes to get Danny to the church, and then she could turn around and head home.

"You are the prettiest girl I know except for my mama. I'm sorry that you are sad and it makes you act mean sometimes."

What? Helen worked to remain composed and respond appropriately. She was comfortable with Danny, but never ready for the things he said. He was a savant of sorts—a wise child—but he possessed absolutely no guile. He was innocent, honest, and totally devoid of tact. "Thank you, Danny. I'm sorry . . . was I mean to you? I didn't mean to be . . ."

Danny reached across the truck cab and gave Helen a pat on the shoulder. "It's okay. You aren't mean to me. And anyway, you only *act* mean sometimes. You aren't mean. I know because I talked to Daddy about it."

Not knowing what to say, Helen opted for nothing and silently urged more speed from the blue truck.

Danny spoke again, as she knew he would. "I know why you're sad."

Certain she didn't want to go there, but not seeing any other choice, Helen asked, "Why, Danny?"

"Because your husband died in the war. That's the main reason."

She nodded. "That's right."

"I know that's why you're sad, but is that why you're mad?"

Helen could feel Danny looking at her and knew he would wait until she answered. "Um . . . Buddy . . . do you want to talk about something else?" *Please!*

"No, thanks."

Helen sighed. She coughed nervously and asked, "Ahhh . . . what was the question?"

Danny spoke slowly as if he was explaining a difficult concept. "I said, 'Your husband died in the war.' Then I said, 'Is that why you are mad?'"

Helen wiped tears that sprang to her eyes and gritted her teeth. *Please, God, make him stop.* "Ahmm . . . Danny . . . yes." She cleared her throat. "I think that does make me mad."

"But who are you mad at?"

At the moment, the answer was quickly becoming "you," but Helen bit her lip and took a deep breath—about to take another stab at leading the conversation in a different direction—when once more, Danny began to talk.

"If you are mad at a soldier, I think you have to forgive him. You want to know why?"

Convinced now that her only option was to endure this torture for a few more minutes, Helen made a mental note never again to get into a vehicle with Danny Gilbert, then answered, "Yes."

"I think you have to forgive him for *you*."

Though she was trying desperately to tune him out, Helen could not help being curious about *this* line of thinking. "Why's that?"

"Because whenever you get hurt by somebody, you can

either think about 'em all day long and let 'em keep hurting you inside . . . or give them to God."

Helen furrowed her brow. "Give them to God?"

"Unh-huh. If you forgive them, it doesn't mean they get away with what they did . . . it just means that *you* don't have to think about it all the time. You can't do anything anyway, except be mad. See? You just give 'em to God. Then you can be happy." With that, Danny smiled and nodded a couple of times, then faced forward in his seat, seemingly satisfied that he had solved his friend's problem.

Helen was grateful for the silence. Give 'em to God . . . then you can be happy. She repeated the words a couple of times in her head and thought, *Yeah, it would be nice if it were that simple.*

She dropped Danny off at the church and headed south toward home. It was so strange, she reflected as she drove, that whole thing about giving them to God. She smiled at a crazy thought: *So what does God do with them when He gets them?* And she laughed at the ridiculous answer that popped into her head: *What do I care? They don't belong to me anymore.*

CHAPTER 10

WHEN HELEN OPENED THE DOOR TO THE COTTAGE, THE first thing she saw was Josef, fully dressed in his uniform, sitting upright on the couch. She entered warily, noticing that he had, at least, possessed the strength to move about. It was apparent that his fever (and presumably its accompanying bewilderment) had faded away. Was he dangerous? Helen might have laughed had she known Josef was asking himself the same question about her.

"Hello," Josef said tentatively.

Helen did not respond, but without taking her eyes off him, she set her purse and keys on the kitchen counter and moved to the sink to draw a glass of water. Noting the water glass in front of Josef on the coffee table, she said, "I would offer you some, but I see you helped yourself."

Josef nodded. "I did. I had hoped you would not mind."

"Found your clothes, did you?"

"Yes, in the washroom. Again, I hope you do not mind that I entered that private area. You were kind to wash my uniform. Thank you." Josef watched curiously as Helen sat down at the kitchen table, not entering the living room where he was, instead keeping her distance. *She is afraid of me,* he thought, *or hates me with passion. Or both.* "May I ask how long I have been here?"

Helen studied his face for any hint of deception. She saw only the black eyes and cut lips. "You don't remember?" He shook his head. "You've been barely conscious for two days. High fever . . ." She shrugged. "I really thought you might die. How's your shoulder?"

Josef glanced toward the wound. "I've never had anything hurt like this in my life, but I looked at it when I put on my uniform and . . . well, it doesn't appear gangrenous . . . you took much care. Again, I thank you."

After a moment, Helen said, "You're welcome." Then, "Are you hungry?"

Actually, Josef admitted, he was famished and soon was balancing a plate of biscuits on his lap. Helen had made them from scratch, not talking to him at all while she cooked. As Josef ate, Helen disappeared into her bedroom, and about the time he had eaten his fill, she reemerged, having changed into slacks and a blue cotton shirt. Barefooted, Helen whisked the empty pan from the coffee table as she passed through the living room on the way to the kitchen.

Josef sat quietly as she washed the plate and placed it back in a cabinet. When Helen finished tidying the kitchen, she wiped her hands on a dish towel, purposefully strode into the living room, and sat down in a chair opposite Josef. She said, "I have some questions."

"All right," Josef replied.

"What is your full name?"

"Josef Landermann. Josef Bartels Landermann."

"How can you speak English so well?"

"I studied English in school . . . and I attended college at Oxford. That's in Eng—"

"I know where Oxford is," Helen snapped.

"Of course," Josef apologized quickly. "I didn't mean to—"

"Who is Tatiana?"

"What? Why?"

"Who is she?" Helen demanded.

As his mind continued to disentangle from its webs of confusion, Josef was becoming increasingly cognizant of the perilous nature of his situation. There existed, in his vastly shrunken world, only one possibility of help . . . and it was this young woman—who had made it abundantly clear that she was *not* his friend. And yet she had saved his life. But for further reasons he could not yet fathom, she had plainly chosen not to alert the authorities to his presence. Would she help him escape? *Escape?* Josef wondered. *What a ridiculous thought! Of course, she will not. Even if she did . . . escape to where?*

Helen leaned forward in her chair. "Who is Tatiana?"

Josef answered politely, but deliberately: "Tatiana is my wife."

"Rosa?"

"My daughter." Josef watched Helen carefully. He had seen her blink at the acknowledgment of his wife and child. Some of the venom had disappeared from her eyes. Now Josef asked a question: "May I ask how you know their names?"

Helen didn't answer at first. She was trying to regain the aggressive posture she'd felt slip at the mention of Josef's family. For some reason, it seemed beyond comprehension that this monster might have a connection to people who valued him, who loved him. "I knew their names," Helen began slowly, "because you have talked to them for two days. You have called out those names again and again."

Josef dropped his head and stared at his hands. After a bit, Helen rose and went into the kitchen. When she returned, she dropped Josef's submariner's pack into his lap. "This was in your pocket," she said without sympathy, but also without the anger that had been there moments before. "Nice picture of you in there, I suppose, and I don't care for the one with Adolf at all, but in light of what you just told me, I am assuming the third photograph is of you, Tatiana, and Rosa."

Josef nodded as he opened the pack and removed the family picture. Blinking back tears, he confirmed Helen's assumption and remarked, "When it was not in my uniform, I took for granted that it had been lost in the water." He added, "I don't mind that you went through it."

Helen cocked her head. "You don't mind? That's big of you."

Josef smiled shyly. "I didn't mean it like that," he said.

Helen almost smiled in return. "I know." She took a deep breath. "We have to change the dressing on your shoulder. Do you have the energy to get up?"

"No, but I will do it if you tell me to."

Helen raised her eyebrows. "Really? You will do whatever I tell you?"

Josef hesitated, then answered affirmatively, but with a slight question in his voice: "Yes?"

Helen motioned with her hand. "Then do it." She didn't help him as he struggled to his feet, but when he finally stood, she gestured to the bathroom. "Go in and take your shirt off."

Helen stepped to retrieve a clean cloth from the kitchen, but turned around when she realized he had not moved. He was pale, she saw. "Are you sick?"

"No . . . I . . ."

Helen furrowed her brow. "What?"

Josef indicated the bathroom, and Helen understood then that he was not sick, but embarrassed. He spoke barely above a whisper: "You want me to go into your private area . . . with you?"

Helen shook her head and smiled in disbelief. "You're married? My God—a half-drowned, shot-up Nazi who is a prude. You are something else." She pointed. "Go. These aren't the Middle Ages, Adolf."

HELEN READ AS JOSEF SLEPT THROUGH THE DAY ON THE COUCH. Redressing the wounds had drained him, and this was the first time Helen had seen him sleep peacefully. She was exhausted, too, though not in the same way. Fear had done Helen in.

She had spent both nights locked in her bedroom, awake, listening to the ravings of a madman, terrified that he might suddenly beat down the door and strangle her. She was mortified that she had not immediately turned him in, was incredulous that she had not, and was now beyond any idea of what to do besides kick him out. Then, there was the offhand possibility that the army might suddenly appear, surround her cottage, and shoot them both.

I could kick him out, Helen thought as she watched Josef snore softly, *but when he is caught—and he will be caught— the trail will lead right back to me. Who cleaned your wounds? Who fed you? Who gave you shelter? Me, me, me.* In the absence of any concept of what to do or which way to turn, Helen made the de facto decision to do nothing.

Earlier in the day, as she worked on his shoulder, Josef

had asked her name. After only a brief hesitation, she obliged him and gave it. *In for a nickel, in for a dime,* she had grimaced later, thinking it was becoming less and less likely she would be able to extricate herself from this incredible mess.

Helen opened her eyes. It was almost dark in the living room, and she realized with a touch of panic that she had fallen asleep. The book was on her chest. She looked across it to see Josef still lying prone, but awake and watching her. She coughed and straightened, unsure about whether she should blush or scream.

"You were very tired," Josef said. "I thought it best to let you sleep."

"At least you didn't crawl over here and cut my throat," Helen said. "That's something, right?"

Josef frowned. "May I say something?" he asked.

"Certainly," Helen answered, placing her book on the floor beside her and folding her hands in her lap. "After all, it is a free country, and although I am sure *you* have never experienced anything like it, while you are a guest of sorts here in America, you might as well take advantage of our customs."

Josef shook his head and sighed. "That is exactly what I wish to comment on."

"What? A free country? You know, if you would—"

"Excuse me," Josef interrupted. Helen's mouth closed. "What I wish to say is this: I appreciate your help. Your actions have been very kind. Your sarcasm, however, is beginning to offend me." Helen angrily sucked in a breath and was about to fire back, but stopped as Josef held up his hand.

"Wait!" he said. "Let me talk for only a brief moment.

Then, if you wish, I will go." He paused to begin again in a calmer voice. "What I mean for you to hear is this: I have no intentions of cutting anyone's throat, I am not a Nazi, and I don't appreciate being called 'Adolf.' I despise the man. I do not understand why I am here, in this country . . . a country that, by the way, I have always admired. It was nothing I planned or anticipated, and I am sincerely sorry for my intrusion into your life.

"If you wish, I will obediently leave and never acknowledge your help. But if I am to stay . . . that is, if you allow me continued refuge until I heal, I humbly request that you refrain from comments about my dark intentions. I have none. I am not a professional military man, despite what my uniform and circumstances would have you believe. I am a high school history teacher, who wanted only to raise a child with my wife.

"I did not choose to fight for my country. And never wanted to fight yours. I was forced to do so. God forbid that you and your countrymen should ever be placed in the position to do the bidding of a madman." Josef relaxed his posture. "Once more, I thank you. Now, do you wish me to leave?"

Helen looked evenly at the man before her but said nothing. She knew she had no intention of throwing him out, yet she was reluctant to let him know that. "You may stay for the time being," she said slowly. "I will avoid commentary, as you have requested, but I still have questions . . . As for your remark about my country doing the bidding of someone like Hitler . . . don't worry about us. It could never happen here."

Josef nodded, but couldn't resist a response. "As I said, 'God forbid,' however, as history tells us: He sometimes does not. In other words, with all due respect . . . don't be so sure."

A WEEK PASSED. JOSEF'S SHOULDER WAS HEALING, AND THOUGH the pain and stiffness had not abated to any great degree, he sensed progress. The wound on his leg, while sore, now amounted to nothing more than a long scab. Even his facial cuts and bruises were clearing.

Helen, Josef worried, had abandoned her social life since he had arrived. It was apparent to him, he said one day, that she did nothing beyond the café and home. He urged her to be careful not to alert anyone else to her change of schedule. She had laughed and told him that she had no social life to abandon, a statement Josef accepted, but found hard to believe.

After all, she was beautiful, Josef admitted to himself, even if she had been frustratingly rude, mean, and generally difficult to like. Over the past few days, however, even that had changed a bit. Helen no longer snarled at him with every sentence, and they had begun to have tentative conver- sations about their lives, nothing serious, but cordial. Helen's questions no longer came wrapped in an accusatory tone, and for that, Josef was grateful.

So far, he had not left the house. He still wore his uni- form—Helen washed it every other day—but he removed the ribbon and U-boat badge, placing it in a buttoned pocket with his Iron Cross and ring. Helen asked to see the items one day, and he let her. "What does this say?" she asked, pointing to the script that wrapped around the ring. They sat, drinking tea, at the kitchen table.

"We sail against England," he said. "The ring was a gift

from my best friend, my commander, Hans Kuhlmann, when I came aboard his boat." As Joseph talked, Helen traced the letters with a fingernail. "We grew up together, Hans and I. He is a good man. Hans loves the Kriegsmarine—navy to you—and is about the business for which he was born, but shares my dislike of Hitler and his so-called High Command."

Josef reached for the ring. Holding it aloft, he said, "We sail against England," and shook his head sadly. "How stupid." He dropped the ring back into his pocket and buttoned it up. "Especially stupid for me . . . I was at Oxford for four years and love everything about the country . . ." Josef grinned suddenly and straightened his back, affecting a haughty expression and then, in a perfect British accent, said, "Love it, I do. Smashing place, what? Fish, chips, Big Ben . . . bloody foggy on occasion, but then, so's my disposition . . . all in all, lovely country."

Helen's eyes opened wide. "Wow!" she exclaimed and genuinely laughed. "That was incredible! How do you do that?"

Josef smiled. "No great talent, really. I've always been able to imitate dialects, sounds, whatever . . ." He shrugged. "If I can hear it, I can do it. Not a useful skill, but it entertained my classmates."

They sat quietly for a while, and for the first time, Josef felt completely at ease with Helen. He had already heard the story of how she came to own this cottage in the middle of nowhere, and although Helen refused to talk about her husband, she seemed fairly forthcoming about other aspects of her life there along the Gulf coast. Josef noticed, however, that despite Helen's ability to be polite when she needed to be and present an occasional smile, there was an anger that bubbled just below her calm demeanor.

Absently Josef flipped through several magazines that were in a small wooden rack beside the table. "Does your government require all publications in America to display your flag on the front cover?"

"What?" Helen scrunched up her face in a puzzled expression, then understood. "Oh, I see what you're asking," she said. "No. No one has required them to do it. They just did. See?" Helen reached across Josef and drew several magazines from the holder and scattered them about the tabletop. Josef saw *Newsweek, Good Housekeeping, Ladies' Home Journal, Glamour,* and *Vogue.* Each cover featured a flag in a scene or standing alone. Josef also noticed the motto "United We Stand" on every one.

"It's July," Helen explained. "This is our country's birthday month, and obviously we are at war . . . anyway, every magazine, comic book, and periodical in the country—more than five hundred of them—made the flag their cover."

"Really?"

"Yep." Helen dug out a few more. "See? Every magazine in America—July 1942—has a flag . . . from *Time* to *Popular Mechanics* to *Life* and *Field and Stream.* They all did it."

"Incredible," Josef murmured.

"It is, isn't it?" Helen affirmed, a hint of pride in her voice. She allowed Josef time to glance through the covers, then spoke, "I want to ask you about something you said the other day."

"Certainly." Josef put down the magazines and focused on Helen.

"You said, 'God forbid that we—our country—should ever be forced to do the bidding of a madman.' I said it would never happen here, and you responded with words to the effect of, 'Don't bet on it.' I don't get the idea you were being a wise guy. I think you were being serious." Helen left the statement as a query, hanging in the air.

"Indeed I was," Josef confirmed and, seizing upon Helen's questioning expression as permission to continue, did so. "History tells us that a democracy is always temporary in nature. It simply cannot exist as a permanent form of government. My country is a classic example. And as a humble, but sincere student of history, I sorrowfully expect your country to one day follow suit."

"Oh, come on," Helen scoffed good-naturedly. To her, it was a statement of such impossibility that it didn't even provoke serious scorn.

Josef shrugged. "This is not my idea, Helen. And it is not a new one. In 1787, Alexander Tyler, a Scottish history professor at the University of Edinburgh, noticed a continuing pattern in the advance and decline of the world's democracies.

"He stated then that a democracy would continue to exist until such time that the voters discover that they can literally vote themselves gifts from the public treasury. From the moment that revelation is made, the majority proceeds to vote for the candidates who promise the most benefits from the public treasury. The final result is that every democracy finally collapses due to loose fiscal policy. That collapse is always followed by a dictatorship.

"Tyler charted the ages of the world's greatest civilizations from the beginning of history . . . an average existence of about two hundred years. Every single time, these nations progressed through the following sequence: from bondage to spiritual faith; from spiritual faith to great courage; from courage to liberty; from liberty to abundance; from abundance to complacency; from complacency to apathy; from apathy to dependence; and finally from dependence back into bondage."

Josef ended and gestured with his hands as if to say, there you are, then added, "Of course, as I said before: God forbid." Helen simply nodded.

CHAPTER 11

"Do you want to walk on the beach?"

Josef turned from the window to face Helen, who had asked the question. "May I?" he responded.

"Josef," she said, "you're not a prisoner. Not that I really know *what* you are."

It was the second week in August, and Josef was becoming restless. The wounds on his shoulder, front and back, were covered with new, pink skin, but the muscle was still weak. Most of the time, he carried his right arm in a sling, more from weariness than pain. He ventured out of the cottage often while Helen was in town, though never farther than the immediate area around her home. Josef had found an old rake in the tool shed under the house and, as best he could with one good arm, cleaned pine straw and brush from the sandy "yard."

"If you want, I'll walk with you. We won't see a soul." Helen pooched out her lips and looked thoughtful. "Still," she said with a point of her finger, "you can't wear that. Even without the medals, it looks like a uniform . . . the wrong uniform. And if we should happen across someone . . . well, your silver buttons give it away."

She went to the closet in the bedroom and pulled a green

canvas bag from its corner. Josef stood at the bedroom door and saw Helen hesitate before opening it. "Do you need help?" he asked.

Helen, on her knees, merely held out her open palm toward him. *Be quiet? Go away? What does she want me to do?* Josef wondered. Then he noticed her tears and retreated into the living room where he sat down and waited.

Soon, Helen emerged from the bedroom. With red eyes and a sniffle, she placed a pair of pants and a shirt on Josef's lap. "They were my husband's," she said. "He didn't wear them much . . . and I'm tired of washing your clothes anyway. There's a whole bag of stuff here. Go through it. Leave his uniform."

Josef hesitated, then asked, "Are you certain you don't mind?"

"No," she replied, striking a somewhat defiant pose, "I am *not* certain I don't mind. But do it anyway. My *husband* wouldn't mind." She shook her head. "That was him . . . Captain Mason . . . always wanting to help. He wouldn't have even been overseas, but he volunteered. Volunteered! Went over to help train British pilots . . ." She shook her head again, a bit more angrily this time. Gesturing to the canvas bag, she indicated her speech was over. "So go through it . . . whatever you need."

Twenty minutes later, the German sailor and the American widow walked the beach, not exactly together, but at the same time. Not yet truly friends, at least they were no longer enemies. Helen had settled in her mind Josef's "difference in a German and a Nazi" and was convinced that he hated Hitler as much as any American. In addition, she had come to believe that Josef was a good man. She marveled at his calm and was impressed by his intelligence and his wisdom.

Each, however frequently they talked (and after all, there was little else to do), had kept much of himself or herself from the other. Despite being free to express an opinion openly for the first time in years, Josef still kept his innermost feelings to himself. He answered candidly when questioned, but offered little.

Helen, for her part, could not escape the sensations of fear and occasional anger that ruled her life. She still felt somewhat guilty about keeping Josef's presence a secret. And even though she had begun to feel comfortable—and strangely comforted—around Josef, her personal history subconsciously cautioned her that he would soon be gone.

Though neither acknowledged the inability to open those final doors to the other's deepest thoughts, the way they communicated displayed proof that this was so. One might say, "May I ask you a question?" instead of just asking it. Or, "If you don't mind my being honest . . ." with a pause, as if somehow one's honesty might not be welcomed or accepted by the other.

For more than an hour, Helen and Josef walked along the shore to the west. Helen pointed out the place she had found him almost a month before. Having grown tired, Josef asked to sit and rest for a bit, and as they did, a final wall between them came tumbling down.

They sat on a dune, silent for a time, each lost in thought. The smell of salt was thick in the warm breeze. Helen was to Josef's right, several feet away, absently drawing in the sand with her foot and keeping an eye on Josef, who seemed to be watching the horizon.

"Looking for submarines?" she asked.

Josef showed the vaguest hint of a rueful smile. "At this moment, submarines are the farthest thing from my mind."

He pulled the top of a sea oat down to his lap without breaking its stalk and ruffled the blooms gently with a finger. "Actually I hope never to see a submarine again." He added, "Though I do hope to see Hans one day. He is truly my friend . . . though I don't know why he left me in the water."

Helen considered this and decided not to comment. Instead she asked, "Do you think about going home?"

"Some," Josef answered, looking once more to the Gulf, "but I do not know how it can be accomplished. Besides, it is not a burning desire."

Helen looked at him sharply, taken aback. "Don't you miss your wife?"

"Of course. You miss your husband, do you not?"

Helen got to her feet in order to look down on Josef with warning in her eyes. Her cheeks flushed. "It's not the same," she said through clenched teeth.

"Why is it not the same?" Josef asked, meeting her gaze.

Helen swallowed the rage rising in her throat. "Because my husband is dead."

"Then it is the same," Josef said as he looked away.

A seagull called nearby as Helen stared at him. The color drained from her face as the comprehension of Josef's words took her breath. "What?" she whispered in disbelief.

A single tear tracked down his face. "My Tatiana . . . my baby Rosa . . . they are dead too."

Helen eased down onto the sand again, closer to Josef, but not touching. "How?" she asked. "When? I mean, you don't have to tell me if—"

"No," he said softly, continuing to look out at the water, "I don't mind." Josef drew a deep, lurching breath to stave off a sob and began.

"I was home—Cologne—on leave. This was, what, only two and a half months ago? Thirty May . . . the night of . . . and I was to depart the next morning. After dinner, I lay on the couch in our apartment. My child, Rosa, went to sleep on my chest . . . her blonde hair was washed. It smelled like . . ." Josef's lip quivered. "My God, she smelled like a baby, you know?" Josef gave an anguished cry, then put his head into his lap and wept. Helen closed her eyes and did not move.

After a moment, Josef wiped his eyes and nose roughly with his hand and coughed, clearing his throat. "I am sorry." He coughed again and seemed to gain a measure of control. "Tatiana took Rosa to her bassinet, then took me to bed. We lay holding each other . . . talking about our only child . . . making promises for more . . .

"Then the planes came. I must have been asleep. Tatiana heard them first. She ran to Rosa, who had begun to cry . . ." Josef's face was turned toward Helen, but his eyes stared past her, seeing the night of his horror all over again. "The sound was . . . strange. It was a hum that shook the air." He paused. "Reports later said there were over one thousand RAF bombers involved in the raid.

"So I ran outside to see what direction the attack was coming from. Where do I take my family? Which way is safety? Then the bombs began to fall." Josef's eyes narrowed, then widened. He looked at Helen. "A bomb shrieks as it falls. Did you know that? Like a woman dying . . . like Tatiana died . . ." Josef's eyes fogged again as once more, he stared past Helen.

"Explosions were everywhere . . . all around me . . . it was quiet, though . . ." He frowned. "It should not have been quiet, but I could not hear. Neither could I see which building was mine . . . which one Tatiana and Rosa were in. Then I realized they were all down . . . all the buildings, I mean." His eyes widened, and he gestured helplessly. "But the bombs kept falling."

Helen wiped the tears from her cheeks as Josef lapsed into silence. A school of jack crevalle, slashing and swirling as they pounded menhaden near the beach, caught the couple's attention for a moment. As the big fish sounded, Josef absently grabbed a handful of sand and sifted it through his fingers as he continued.

"The bombing lasted only two hours, though it seemed much longer than that." Josef shook his head disgustedly. "And I was unharmed. We—the people left alive—could no longer recognize anything. There were no landmarks standing . . . it was not dark, of course—everything was on fire. It was as I've always imagined hell.

"I called for Tatiana . . . the night was filled with voices at that point. No one begging for help. Just hundreds of voices crying out names of lost loved ones . . ." Josef's tears began again to flow. His eyes were open as he looked toward the sky. In the afternoon heat, Helen shivered as he murmured the names he remembered hearing that night. "Chloe . . . Gabrielle . . . Martin . . . Deidre . . . Bernhard . . . Suzanne . . ."

He paused. "I began to dig through the rubble at dawn. It was almost noon when I found Tatiana. Rosa was in her arms." He looked at Helen, an uncomprehending expression on his face, and said, "They were broken, but together. They were not bleeding anymore . . . they had no more blood . . ." He held his arms out helplessly. "They were just . . . gone. I told them I was sorry . . . that I loved them . . . but they were gone."

His face grew dark. "The Gestapo came then and pulled me up. They made me leave. They said my responsibility was to the Führer." Then, collapsing completely, Josef wailed, "I was not allowed to bury them! I did not say good-bye!" He fell sideways into the sand and wept bitterly.

Tears cascading down her face, Helen moved close to Josef and placed her hand on his back. She did not pat him or even press firmly. She didn't speak at all, for her emotions were too unsure. Helen knew only that she felt his anguish and was compelled to convey her understanding in some way.

When at last Josef gained control, he rolled over onto his back. Looking up at Helen, he said, "I know I must forgive. I can only hope it gets easier than it is at present to do so."

Helen frowned. "What do you mean?"

"I mean, we are products of our past, but we don't have to be prisoners of it."

Helen shook her head impatiently. "No. I meant, what do you mean when you say, 'I know I must forgive'?"

"Just that I must practice forgiveness. It is less an act than a determined way of living. I think that is why we are supposed to forgive 'seventy times seven.' True forgiveness comes only at the conclusion of an inner struggle."

"Josef," Helen said, "I am not making myself clear. What I want to know is, why are you talking about forgiveness at all?"

Josef looked surprised. "Well, I suppose because it occurs to me that you and I both need to forgive the same thing." When Helen didn't respond, Josef tried to clarify his last statement. "Germans killed your husband . . . and in a way, I guess Americans killed my wife."

Helen was stunned. "What? That is the . . . I can't believe

you would even . . ." She was sputtering. Her mouth opened and closed. She was getting angrier by the second. Pointing her finger in Josef's face, she hissed, "*You* are a German soldier . . . sailor, whatever. *You* killed my husband. He was an American. He had *nothing* to do with the death of your wife. The RAF bombed Cologne. You said so yourself!"

Having listened to her words without reaction, he calmly got up and brushed the sand from his clothes. Before turning and walking back down the beach by himself, Josef withered Helen with a glare and said, "Yes, the RAF bombed Cologne. And your husband trained the RAF. Remember? You said so yourself."

THE BEDROOM FAN'S CALMING HUM WAS ENOUGH MOST NIGHTS to promptly ease Margaret into a restful sleep. The fan, set into the window by the chest of drawers, was a constant in her life, an audible assurance every evening that things were as they should be.

Once, several years ago, Margaret and Billy had left Danny with a neighbor and traveled to New Orleans for the only vacation either of them had taken since their honeymoon. It was to have been three glorious days and nights at the Fairmont, a ridiculously expensive hotel near the French Quarter, but a hotel, they discovered, without a window fan. The five-bladed wicker fan turning lazily in the ornate hotel room's ceiling was beautiful and did indeed move the air, but left the bedroom as silent as a tomb. After two sleepless nights, the couple checked out of the Fairmont and went home to Foley, Danny, and their noisy window fan.

Margaret turned from her side onto her back and looked into the darkness. After only a moment, she sat up to straighten the sheet, then lay back down. Soon she was again on her side. When a problem weighed on her mind, Margaret was generally unable to drift off, and this night had been no different in that respect. And the fan had not helped.

"Are you asleep?" she whispered to her husband.

In a full voice that startled her and indicated that, no, he was not, Billy answered, "Rip Van Winkle couldn't sleep in this bed. I'm having to hold on to the mattress to keep from being bounced out!"

Margaret chuckled and snuggled close to him. "I'm sorry."

Billy put his arm around her and said, "That's all right. What's wrong? We gotta get up before too long, so you might as well tell me."

Margaret sighed. "Has Danny asked you anything about Helen lately?"

"Um-hmm. Three or four times. You know how he is . . ."

"Yeah, he's been after me about it too."

"The 'why is Helen mean' thing?"

"That seems to be the subject." Margaret stuffed her pillow behind her back and sat up. The hall light, left on every night for Danny, mitigated the darkness and allowed Billy to see the concern on his wife's face as she spoke. "Have you talked to him about forgiveness?"

"Yeah. Why?"

"Because that's what he has been asking me about." Margaret thought for a bit, then said, "You know, we've talked about this before. Danny feels things other people don't. It's strange, isn't it? Sweet? How he's so concerned about her, I mean?"

"Well, why wouldn't he be?" Billy said as he arranged

his own pillow behind his back and sat up to join Margaret. "You're concerned about her, and that shows. I am too. She's a good girl. But, Margaret, you *know* . . . we been through this ourselves . . . forgiveness is a hard deal if you don't understand it. And some people—like me and you were at one time—are so mad about the past that they can't see the future. Forgiveness is letting go of the past."

Margaret shook her head. "Well, I haven't said anything to her about it in a while."

"You can't. You don't know what she's upset about, really. I mean, it's all tied up with her husband getting killed . . . but beyond that, what do we really know?"

"Nothing, I guess. I just wish I could grab her and shake her and tell her the truth. If she were a daughter of mine . . ."

"Which she ain't . . ."

"I know, but if she were a daughter of mine, I could talk about this kind of thing with her."

"Margaret. It'll come in time. Be her friend."

"I just want to tell her the truth about what her life can be like if she 'gets' this."

Billy reached over and grabbed his wife. Pulling her into a hug, he said, "Sweetheart . . . Helen's having a hard time with the pain. She's got a good friend in you, and I know you're all full of 'the truth shall set you free.' And it will. But sometimes . . . first, it can make you miserable. That's where she's at. Give her time."

Even though they remained in a sitting position, Billy dozed off in the silence that followed. Margaret was careful not to move, her husband's arm still around her, as she listened to his soft snoring. She smiled. Billy was a wise man, Margaret knew. He was well-read and smart as a whip, though she teased him about his manner of speaking that often, she laughed, kept his intelligence a "secret." Billy said "ain't," "me and you," "anyways," and made no apology for his speech, but as terrible as Billy's grammar could be, years ago, his "language" was infinitely worse. Margaret lay her head on Billy's shoulder and remembered the day that changed.

Billy had been well-known in Baldwin County for his creative use of oaths, expletives, and the intermittent obscenity. It was said that he could cuss a streak that often displayed many shades of blue. Curiously, however, this never, ever occurred in the presence of a lady. Or Danny.

One afternoon over coffee, Margaret had asked him about that anomaly, and he'd responded with a grin. "First thing I want to know is . . . ," he said, "how do you even know I swear?" She confessed that she had overheard him with other men on occasion. Billy had nodded apologetically and rationalized, "First of all, my daddy talked that way . . . That ain't no excuse and I know it, but somehow, I guess I feel close to my daddy when I talk like he did.

"I don't talk that way in front of Danny 'cause it's a bad example. He's a child. And also because I don't want 'sorry language' that he hears in the future to remind him of his daddy the same way 'sorry language' reminds me of mine. The reason I don't cuss in front of ladies is respect. Respect for them . . . respect for you. Anyhow, that's why I don't swear in front of women and kids."

At that point, Margaret had taken a sip of her coffee and maintained eye contact with her husband, saying nothing. "You think that's a crock, don't you?" he asked.

She smiled. "Do you want some more coffee?" she said simply.

"You think all I just said is a d-a-m stupid reason for cussing, is that right?"

Margaret ducked her head and averted his gaze. Trying desperately not to laugh out loud, she almost blew coffee through her nose when he spelled the word instead of saying it in front of her—and spelled it incorrectly! Slowly Margaret looked up to find Billy, bug-eyed, veins bulging, leaning across the table as if daring her to disagree.

That had done it. Somehow, it was the funniest thing she had ever seen. Like laughing in church or at a funeral, Margaret had known it was a terribly inappropriate response, but she just couldn't help it. Worse, every time she attempted to calm herself, she glanced at Billy, saw his exaggerated expression of patient "hurt feelings," and dissolved into another fit of laughter. Before too long, it had become funny to Billy as well, and both had laughed until they were exhausted.

Margaret reached to take Billy's hand and gently squeezed it three times. One . . . two . . . three. I . . . love . . . you. She closed her eyes. Over time, spelling the occasional curse word was enough to get them giggling like teenagers, but spelling was as far as it went.

On that day so long ago, she had not challenged him, had not demanded, mocked him, threatened, or pouted. Margaret had asked her husband a question with an honest smile and was prepared to love him no matter the answer. And to everyone's astonishment, Billy Gilbert had never cursed again.

The laughter was a bonus, Margaret thought as she drifted to sleep in her husband's arms. And it had lasted through the years.

Billy and Margaret seemed ordinary in all respects, but as the seasons in their lives had passed, both had come to understand fully how *extraordinary* they had become together. Margaret possessed a gift of discernment and intuition upon which Billy had come to rely. Billy, for his part, provided logic and wise counsel. Whenever Margaret began to wrap her mind around a concept or a feeling and fully explore its implications, Billy's role was to add comments, ask questions, and organize their conclusions into a clear, larger view.

When they had gotten married, it was a discouraging shock—terrifying, really—to discover how incompatible they seemed, how truly different from each other they were, and they had almost divorced. But slowly they came to respect those differences, even rely upon them, until at last, in a blinding flash of the obvious, Billy and Margaret arrived at an amazing conclusion: If we were just alike . . . one of us would be unnecessary.

When the breaking dawn lightened the bedroom's east window, Billy slipped out of the bed. Soon he was back with coffee and a plate of buttered, toasted biscuits. "Hey, Sugarbear?" He nudged Margaret and presented the spare breakfast to her as she woke up. "Special surprise," he whispered, "today only . . . I put cinnamon on 'em. You better eat a couple before I get Danny up. We need to get going. It's coming up on six."

Margaret got out of bed without a word and quickly brushed her hair. Taking a bite of the reheated biscuit that had been baked at the café the day before, she listened to Billy as he awakened their son. "Buddy Boy! Time to roll, Son! Let's go!"

Margaret shook her head as she heard Danny chuckle and gave silent thanks that the young man was like his father in the way he greeted the morning. God knew, she wished she was. Early in their marriage, however, she had thrown a finger in her husband's face one morning and said, "Listen carefully . . . yelling and loud is not the way I want to wake up. Clowns, insane people, and *you* may do it that way, but I don't!" And from that point on, she had never had to.

Billy came back into their bedroom. "More coffee?" he whispered.

"You can talk now," Margaret said wryly.

"Oh, okay," Billy said in a normal tone and with a total lack of sarcasm, "you want more coffee?"

"No, thanks. I'm fine." She turned around. "Billy, get this middle button, please. I can't ever reach it." Billy stood behind her and quickly did as she asked. "Thank you."

As Billy got dressed, Margaret sat at her vanity table and put on her makeup. "Honey?" she asked. "Who said, 'No man is an island'?"

"You think I don't know?" Billy grinned.

"No . . . So, who said it?"

"John Donne. Sixteenth-century minister."

She shot him a quizzical expression. "How *do* you know that?"

"My mama used to say it. Why are you thinking about 'no man is an island'?"

Margaret brushed some color into her cheeks and said, "Because I think it's only partly correct."

When she didn't continue, Billy finished combing his hair—always the last thing he did before leaving the house—and leaned against the wall beside her. "Explain."

She frowned. "'No man is an island' means that we all need each other . . ."

"True . . . ," Billy prompted.

"But in a way, doesn't that place us at the mercy of

someone else's actions? Aren't there some choices we can make that don't require the participation of others—especially if they hate us?"

Billy was trying to follow his wife's reasoning. "For instance?" he said.

She shoved her makeup back into a drawer and turned to face him. "For instance, whatever Helen's going through . . . Granted, this is nothing anyone ever seems to consider, but isn't Helen an island, so to speak, if she chooses to forgive?"

Billy pondered the question, then said deliberately, "If you mean that we are an 'island' when we choose to forgive because it is not necessary anyone else be involved in the process . . . then, yes, I think you are right."

Warming to the thought, Margaret asked, "Billy, where is it written that for one person to forgive another, the offender must *ask* for forgiveness? Where is it written—not in the Bible, for sure—that for one person to forgive another, the offender must *deserve* it?" Margaret stood. Eyes narrowed, head cocked, she asked, "How about this . . . where is it written that for one person to forgive another, the offender has to approve it, accept it, or even know about it?

"Look at it this way . . . 'No man *is* an island' if we choose *not* to forgive. *Not* to forgive means we yield ourselves to another person's control—another person's governing values and *his* attitudes and actions. We are forced by someone else into sequences of act and response, of outrage and revenge, and you know what? It always gets worse. Our present, when we refuse to forgive, is endlessly overwhelmed by the past. But we become an 'island' when we forgive. The act sets us apart from the burdens of people we generally don't like in the first place! Forgiveness frees the forgiver.

"Sometimes we attach our entire lives to the moment we were hurt and allow it to define and consume our very existence. We travel with that hurt—that offense—and brood over it every time it comes to mind. We sleep with it, eat with it. The 'wrong' that has been done to us dictates how we speak to our children, our spouses, our friends . . .

"Even when those who have mistreated us, abused us, cheated us, or oppressed us . . . my God, Billy, even when *they* die, our anger and resentment do not have the decency to do the same! Our hurt continues to live."

"Until we forgive." Billy nodded. "I see it. There is no such thing as managing one's anger. It simply can't be done. The only answer is to forgive . . . and get rid of it forever."

CHAPTER 12

THE FOLLOWING MORNING, EVERYONE AT THE CAFÉ WAS talking about the blackout. Finally, though without specifically mentioning why, the Feds had issued a proclamation requiring all coastal structures to cover their windows and doors at night. Black paper or cloth was suggested as best suited for the task. And this was no voluntary exercise—the blackout was mandatory and would be enforced by the local sheriff's department.

"More work for you, ain't it, Wan?" one of the regulars called out to the deputy, who sat at the counter with Billy.

Wan grinned. "Can't work more than twenty-four a day," he said, "and that's what they got me doing now." The group laughed as Wan turned back and finished his eggs.

"What *are* you supposed to do?" Billy asked quietly. "Anything different from what you're already doing?"

The deputy shrugged. "Not much. The sheriff said he wants us out of the cars now . . . so I guess that's different. We have to actually walk around the house or business or whatever. I'm headed out today . . . supposed to talk to the owner of the structure or, failing that, post a written order on the door about the whole deal. Then we do some night checks next week to make sure everybody's complied. That's the idea anyway." Billy nodded as Wan wiped his mouth and stood up. As he counted out the change for his breakfast, the deputy, as casually as he could, asked, "What time does Helen come in today?"

"About ten thirty," Billy responded smugly. "Same time she comes in every day she ain't workin' breakfast. You'll see her, Wan, don't worry."

"Oh, I'm not worrying. Just, you know, making conversation. I'll probably be back for lunch."

"Yessir," Billy grinned. "I'll bet you will."

"Oh, shut up," Wan said, embarrassed, and Billy laughed.

"Hello, Wan!" Danny came from the kitchen to stand near his father. "Where are you going today?"

"Beach road, Danny. Starting up with the blackout stuff. You heard, right?"

"I heard," Danny said, his eyes wide with excitement. "Can I go with you today, Wan?"

"Danny . . . ," Billy started, with an apologetic glance at Wan.

"It's okay actually," the deputy said to Billy. "That is, if you don't mind." Sensing his friend's hesitation, but seeing Danny's hopeful expression, Wan sought to make Billy more at ease with the idea. "The sheriff'll be fine with it. He knows Danny, and so does just about everybody we'll be seeing. It's gonna be mostly a lot of walking around. Everybody who lives out there drives trucks. I can't get the squad car stuck so I'll be walking in from the main road in almost every place."

"Please, Daddy," Danny begged. "I can help Wan. Please?"

Billy looked at Wan, who said, "We'll be back in time for

him to help at lunch . . . he'll be great company for me."

"All right, go," Billy said. "But you listen to Wan and do what he says."

The deputy grinned as Danny jumped into the air, hugged his father, then calmed immediately. "Let's do it, Wan," he said.

Billy shook his head and went back to work. He had heard his son asking Wan about the siren as they left and hoped the two were at least out of earshot before the deputy allowed Danny to turn it on.

A short time later, the two were turning off Highway 3 and onto the Beach road. "Who do we get to talk to?" Danny asked.

"Every-single-body," Wan replied. "We'll start right up here at these houses on the lagoon, then on out all the way to Fort Morgan . . . you've been there, right?"

"Unh-huh. I go with my daddy sometimes."

"We need to hit every house, cottage, and squatter's cabin between here and the fort," Wan said. "That includes the bay side . . . Navy Cove, where old Harris Kramer is . . . and anything else over there."

"My daddy doesn't like Harris Kramer," Danny said. "My daddy spelled a word about Harris Kramer to my mama, but I don't know what it was."

"Anyway . . . ," Wan drew the word out to get Danny's attention back to the subject. "I need *you*, Danny boy, to be looking—"

"My daddy sings that song to me," Danny interrupted.

"What?" Wan was confused.

"'Danny Boy.' My daddy sings that song to me. Oh, Danny Boy. He makes me and Mama laugh. It's a song about pipes. Do you know what pipes are?"

"Ahhh . . . yes. Danny, I need *you* to look closely through—"

"Pipes are things you play songs on."

"That's right," Wan said. "That's exactly right." He took a breath. "Now . . . Danny . . . what I need *you* to do . . . is watch through the woods as we drive along. We can't miss a house, okay?"

"Okay, Wan. I'll look very closely."

"Good man."

"Wan, are we going to Helen's house?"

"Yep," Wan answered. "But I don't think Helen will be there. By the time we get out that far, she'll have already gone to work."

Danny brightened. "But we will pass her! She will come this way, and we will be going that way! We can wave."

"Maybe, buddy," Wan said. "But don't be disappointed if we don't see her. We're likely to miss each other. We'll be off the main road most of the time. We'll drive in as far as we can, but it's all walking from there." Wan pulled the squad car off the road and under some huge live oaks. Shutting its engine off, he slapped Danny on the knee and said, "You ready?"

Danny nodded energetically and opened his door. "Not the kind that have water in them," he said.

Wan, halfway out the squad car, leaned back in and looked through at the earnest young man. "What?" he asked.

"The pipes are not for water. They are for playing."

IN LESS THAN TWO HOURS, WAN AND DANNY HAD COVERED fourteen houses on the lagoon—most of those near the area called Shellbanks—five cottages in the beach dunes and two squatters' cabins Wan had known about that were back in the pines. They also visited the folks at Callaway's Grocery, a tiny cinder block building, and posted a sign on the one-room Lagoon Baptist Church, which of course was empty on a weekday.

Most of the homes were occupied that morning, and the two young men were offered coffee or milk or cake at almost every one. Even the family at the second squatter's cabin—the first had been deserted—presented a hot pan of cornbread. Wan claimed a full stomach, which was true, but more likely did not wish to take food from the mouths of a family in obvious need.

There were several squatters' cabins scattered throughout the area, most in the lagoon swamp or some other out-of-the-way location. These structures ranged from simple lean-tos to much larger, old home sites that had fallen into disrepair and been abandoned. Families who had been devastated financially or those who had never recovered from the Depression—and of those, there were many—took over the cabins, usually for short periods as they traveled on, in search of better times.

For their part, the locals did not seem to mind the transient population. They understood that they were not criminals or "trash," but people who had simply experienced a tough run of luck. In addition, the squatters usually left the structures improved in some way when they departed. It was a traditional expression of gratefulness to which most adhered. A matter of pride, it was also a way to "pay the bill" and ready the structure for the next person or family who came along.

Wan parked the squad car at the entrance to Helen's

property. "Here we go again, Danny," he said. "You making it?"

Danny wiped his forehead with his arm and smiled. "I'm making it."

"This is Helen's house," Wan said as he reached into the backseat for a blackout notice. "She won't be home, so we'll just leave this on her door. Sorry we have to walk in, but there ain't no way this car'll make it through her driveway."

"Too much sand, huh?"

"Yes, sir, too much sand."

As they trudged toward the cottage, Danny asked, "Why don't we just give Helen her paper when we see her at lunch?"

Wan glanced at his pocket watch. It was almost time to head that way. "Well, Danny, that'd be a good idea, but the sheriff made us promise to go to every house in person."

"Okay. Have you ever been to Helen's house before? I came once with Mama and Daddy. Helen had an aunt named Jean. I called her Miss Jean, even though she was old—"

Wan stopped suddenly and put his hand out to halt Danny. "Hush," he said.

"What's wrong?" Danny was puzzled.

"Danny, be real quiet." They had just come around the last curve in the long driveway. The cottage was still seventy-five yards or so in the distance, and Wan was staring intently at it. Without thinking, the deputy loosened the pistol in his holster and eased to one knee, bringing Danny down with him.

There was someone—a man—underneath Helen's house. He was moving . . . doing something . . . looking for something. Wan watched, unable to see clearly because of the distance and the cottage's vertical support pilings that obscured his view. *Who is this?* Wan thought. *What is he holding? Is that a rifle in his hands? Shotgun?*

Locals, extremely respectful of another person's property, rarely ventured in or around someone's home without permission; therefore, an unannounced guest was likely to be suspected of ill intent. *This guy,* Wan thought, *seems unannounced.*

"Danny," Wan said quietly, "do you see that man?" Danny nodded yes, staring. "Do you recognize him?" This time, Danny shook his head no. Wan thought for a moment, then asked, "Danny, has Helen said anything about having a visitor?"

"No," Danny whispered.

"Danny?" Wan spoke quietly, but with intensity. He was trying to watch the man at the cottage, keep still, and look into Danny's eyes at the same time. "Danny, I want you to stay right here, you hear me? Do not move. Don't move 'til I call you, okay?" Danny continued to look toward the house. Wan popped him on the shoulder. "Danny, okay?"

"Okay," Danny said, but before the deputy could move, he grabbed his arm. "Wan, is that a bad man?"

"I don't know. Stay here, okay? I mean it."

"Okay," Danny said again.

Wan slipped into the trees to his right and eased around a large dune. His intention was to get closer to the house. After carefully stepping through a large clump of palmettos and trying not to think about how many rattlesnakes he'd seen in bushes just like these, the deputy moved across a thick stand of scrub oak and stopped to get his bearings. *Fifteen yards off the drive. Dune line paralleling the beach. How close am I?*

Wan silently climbed the dune and peeked his head over the top. He was almost thirty yards closer. *Forty yards to the house,* Wan calculated, *maybe forty-five . . .* The man was still there, but he had his back to the deputy and was on the other side of all those pilings. Wan squinted. The sun was almost overhead, leaving the man in shadow. It was tough to see. *What has he got in his hands? Not hands. Hand. Whatever it is, he's carrying it with one hand. Like I carry my rifle. Oh, Jesus . . . it's a rifle. I think.*

Before moving again, Wan glanced to where he had left Danny . . . and froze. Danny was not there. Sticking his head up higher than he knew he should—especially since a guy with a rifle was less than fifty yards away—Wan scanned the brushy area desperately for Danny. Where was he? There. *No, no, no! Danny, Danny!* Wan scrambled furiously down the dune. Danny was creeping down the drive path toward the cottage!

Which way? At the bottom of the dune, Wan had to instantly choose whether to continue around the mountain of sand and attempt to intercept Danny before he was seen—or to go back the way he came and grab the young man from behind. *Back,* he decided and rushed in that direction.

Wan was in the oak clearing when he heard the voice from the cabin. He didn't understand what had been said, but it had been loud enough . . . the man could have only been addressing Danny—the boy had obviously been spotted. The deputy tore through the palmetto thicket, dropping all pretense of stealth.

Drawing his gun, Wan could see Danny through the trees and brush. The young man was now standing straight up, no longer trying to hide. He was looking at whoever had called out and was right in the middle of the driveway—like a deer in the headlights. Wan heard the man call out again. He struggled to see . . . and there he was. Wan caught a glimpse here and there . . . The man was moving swiftly.

Wan took one quick step to his right and got his pistol up. Still the man came. *He doesn't know I'm here. Danny! Move! Run!* Wan's heart was about to come out of his chest. His breathing was ragged and so loud that he was afraid the man might hear him. He saw the stranger more clearly now . . . or at least the top of him, from the shoulders up. The brush between them was still much too thick. *Come on,* Wan thought. *Let me see the rifle, man.*

The stranger stopped less than five yards from Danny, but the positioning couldn't have been more advantageous for the deputy. Wan was no more than seven or eight yards away, he had not been spotted, and he had a clear shot at the guy's head.

Wan could see the fear on Danny's face and remembered the boy's earlier question: "Is that a bad man?" The deputy silently eased back the hammer on the big .45 and thought, *If he's a bad man, he's a dead man.*

Wan Cooper had never really wanted to be a deputy. It was just one of those things that had happened. Growing up, he'd wanted to be a doctor, but that took college and, well, when his father died, Wan wasn't even able to finish high school. Being the oldest, and the only boy, he went to work in order to support his mother and three sisters.

Wan hired himself out to farmers and managed to keep the family fed and clothed, but at nineteen when Harper Gilley, one of his father's old friends, had been elected sheriff, he sensed an opportunity. Wan applied for and was accepted as one of Sheriff Gilley's three deputies. And he'd been a deputy ever since.

When the war started, Wan had wanted to enlist, but was persuaded to serve his country in a domestic uniform. He felt guilty about that, in a way. It was safer, he knew, and that bothered him, but with a sister still in school—and her brother wanting to keep her there—Wan remained on the payroll of the Baldwin County Sheriff's Department, passing out the occasional speeding ticket and driving the squad car in a parade or two every year.

Wan thought it strange, as he gripped the revolver with both hands and sighted down its barrel, that it should occur to him *now* that he had never shot anyone. Except for snakes beside the road or target practice out on some stretch of empty beach, he had never even had the gun out of its holster. And it all seemed to be happening so fast.

"What's your name?" Wan thought he heard the stranger ask the young man in front of him, but Danny cried out and ran. What the man yelled after that, Wan had not been able to understand. However, when the stranger put the rifle under his arm and pointed it at the fleeing boy, Wan pulled the trigger. And missed.

The stranger turned, his mouth open in astonishment. Wan was about to fire again when he realized the man's hands were high in the air. Still pointing his revolver and never taking his eyes off his target, the deputy stepped carefully through the brush to the cleared driveway.

"Move!" Wan roared.

"Fine. Where?" the man replied in a funny voice.

A funny voice? Wan yelled again. "Move! Move! Step away from the . . ." *Rake?* Wan lowered the pistol a fraction. He looked again. Yes, he determined . . . there was a rake at this man's feet. And not a particularly "rifley" looking rake, either. Just your ordinary, everyday rake.

Another thing, Wan noticed. The guy had his arm in a sling. *This will not play well at the café . . . Oh, boy,* he thought, *I shot at a cripple with a rake.*

As calmly as he could manage, Wan lowered his gun. "I'm . . . sorry." It sounded ridiculous, he knew, but it was the only thing he could think of to say. "I thought you had a rifle." The man's eyes widened. "Oh, man. I am sorry."

"That's quite all right."

There's that funny voice again. "Are you hurt . . . Ahhh . . . sir?"

"'Sir,' is it now? No, no. What's done is done. No longer a challenge."

Wan placed his pistol back into its holster. "Really . . . I am *really* sorry. I mean, I know sorry doesn't even begin to cover—"

"I'm fine. Truly I am. Don't give it another thought."

Wan frowned. "You sure are taking this well, you know? After all . . . I shot at you."

The man raised his eyebrows and smiled. "Yes! Yes, you did. But you missed. And aren't we all grateful for that slight deviation in your plan?"

Wan was shaking now and had broken into a cold sweat. "If you don't mind," he said, "I think I'm gonna sit down here for a minute."

"Yes, yes. You go right ahead. May I bring you some water . . . tea perhaps . . . from the cottage?"

"Water would be fine," Wan said. "Thank you." He thought he might throw up.

Josef was no less a bundle of nerves than the deputy as he walked toward the cottage. He was simply a better actor than Wan. The shot had scared him half to death. It was the last thing he had expected.

He had been raking under and around the cottage when he had looked up and seen a man standing in the driveway. Josef's first inclination, of course, had been to flee, but a swift dose of common sense, delivered just in time from who knew where, led him to choose a course of action that would appear much less guilty. *Smile and wave,* he had told himself, and that's just what he had done. He had also maintained the presence of mind not to speak in his normal voice with its Germanic dialect, so again, thinking quickly, Josef had called out a greeting in a crisp British brogue.

Josef had been confused and even more unnerved when the man standing in the driveway had not responded. But knowing he must carry on with what he had begun, Josef continued toward him. It was not until he was much closer that Josef realized that the man—a young man, it turned out—was mentally retarded. It was also apparent that he was terrified, though why . . . Josef had been uncertain.

What did I say that frightened him so badly? Josef wondered as he entered the cottage and retrieved two glasses from the cupboard. *What did I say?* He couldn't remember.

Josef glanced out the window at the deputy. The other young man had returned and was now sitting with him. The two had moved into a patch of shade. Josef got another glass, filled all three, and headed back outside. His right arm still in the sling, he held the glasses against his chest with the left.

Be careful with these men, Josef told himself as he descended the steps. *Remember to play the part . . . you are a Brit.* And in the time it took Josef to approach the two and give them the water, he had invented the beginnings of a whole new life.

"Thank you," Wan said as he took a long swallow. "I am really sorry."

Josef eased himself down into a sitting position and smiled. "Please! Best forgotten. Certainly by me, aye? I absolutely insist . . . no more apologies." Wan responded with a look that expressed his relief and gratefulness.

Josef turned to Danny and suddenly remembered what he had asked before the world had turned upside down. "Now then," he said, "seeing as how we've diminished the risk of another loud bang like the one that followed my question moments ago, permit me to ask again . . . what is your name?"

Wan flushed, knowing this was only the first of what was certain to be a lifetime of sarcastic grenades casually tossed in his direction when this got out. Danny, however, did not notice the jab. He answered with his full name, "Danny Gilbert," and threw out a comment of his own. "You sure do talk strange."

Josef chuckled good-naturedly, though his heart rate had picked up a bit. The deputy, he saw now, was also staring at him with curiosity. "Yes, well, I would, wouldn't I?" Josef managed to bluster. "Not from around here. No, no. But then, you'd have guessed that, I'm thinking. Is that right, Danny?" He held out his hand. "Pleased to make your acquaintance. I'm Josef. Josef Bartels."

The name Landermann, Josef had quickly decided, sounded much too German, while Bartels seemed a bit more British, didn't it? Danny shook his hand, and Josef swung it to Wan, who also accepted the gesture and gave his name.

"The Oxford Bartels," Josef continued. "Yes, Oxford. Lovely place. All the Bartels from London originally, of course, but then . . . weren't we all?" he said with a wink. Josef laughed loudly, causing Wan and Danny to smile politely, though they hadn't the slightest clue what was supposed to be funny or what the man was even talking about.

"Yes, well, so," Josef continued babbling, not really sure what he was talking about, either, but knowing instinctively that he was performing for his life. "The family made its name in Oxford. That's why we are known collectively as the Oxford Bartels . . . Perhaps you've heard of us?" Wan and Danny shook their heads. "No? Well, not surprising, I suppose, what? After you and the colonies went your own way, there really wouldn't be a reason to keep up with a history that wasn't yours now, say?" Josef laughed loudly again and slapped his knee. He was exhausting himself, or more likely, he thought wildly, cracking under the strain. Fortunately Wan spoke, allowing Josef to gather the wits he had left and at least take a breath.

"You know," the deputy began, "with all that's happened, I don't mean to be rude . . . or overly suspicious . . . but are you a guest at this house?" While flustered and embarrassed by his mistake, Wan was aware of his duty and had not entirely let down his guard. He had purposely phrased his question so as not to reveal the owner's name. *Let this guy come up with it,* he thought, *if he can.*

Josef fairly bubbled in reply. "Ah! Hah! Guest, is it?" He slapped his knee again. "Dear friend, more like. Not of Helen, mind you, no. But of her departed aunt Jean, God rest her. Friend of me mum's, she was." Josef leaned in conspiratorially. "I did not know the woman was gone." He rocked back. "Did . . . not . . . know." Josef popped his lips. "Me own mum dead for a year as well . . . war on . . . no news. Me trapped here . . . hurt . . ." Josef indicated his arm in the sling. "Yes, and dear Helen . . . who knew? Honestly I had no idea Jean had a niece." He frowned at Wan. "In any case, she was never mentioned by Mum . . ." Josef brightened again. "Lo then, what? She has been an angel, say? Allowed me the couch and all that . . ."

The tension was transforming Josef into a thespian of rare skill—a talent, he was vaguely aware, that might actually provide freedom . . . or an appointment with a firing squad. The more he chattered, however, casting his British gibberish—"What? Say? Hah! Right!"—the more relaxed (and amused) he saw the deputy becoming. Soon they were all chuckling together.

During their conversation, and in answer to their queries, Josef filled in more blanks. He had been working in New York, unable to get home because of wartime, wanted to see his mother's friend, and was injured in a traffic accident on the way. He had only arrived last week, gratefully accepting Helen's generous offer of shelter . . . and only then because she was family, in a way, and he was hurt.

Every word out of his mouth, of course, was a lie. And in some cases more than others, Josef was aware that each untruth was his potential undoing. He simply did not possess the knowledge of how things were done in America to a degree that might allow him to fabricate his background flawlessly.

For instance, Josef had no idea about whether America allowed her citizens to travel freely during this time. What about foreign citizens? Should he have been able to sail or fly back "home" to England? He had not a clue. His biggest worry, however, was whether Helen could (or would) back up his claims if the deputy saw her before he did. And Josef assumed that he would.

If she were put to the test, Helen would be forced to deal with questions whose answers *he* had concocted. How long has he been here? Where is he from? How was he hurt? He knew you how? From where? The questions demanded answers that she could not ever hope to divine by logic, for Josef had conjured them from that flimsiest of substance— thin air. Suddenly Josef was more frightened than he had ever been in his life, but oddly not for himself. He was frightened for Helen.

HELEN WAS IN THE KITCHEN WITH MARGARET WHEN WAN AND Danny walked into the café. She had asked as to Danny's whereabouts when she had arrived, was told that he was with the deputy—but not where they had gone—and thought no more about it. When Helen met Wan's gaze, however, she felt a chill. Something was wrong. He didn't smile or wave a greeting. Neither did he frown. Wan simply looked at her.

But what Helen identified as growing panic was merely a precursor to the real thing. Moments later, true terror bloomed within her when Danny bounced into the kitchen and, having hugged his mother, said, "Hey, Helen! Wan and me went to your house. We met your friend."

CHAPTER 13

WAN TOOK A SEAT AT THE TABLE BY THE DOOR, ACROSS from the register, and leaned back against the wall. Helen glanced at him again. He was still looking at her. *Is he watching me? What has he done with Josef? Am I about to be arrested?* Helen's first impulse was to dash out the back door and run for the truck, but no, she was sure Wan had covered that means of escape.

"What's wrong with Wan?" Margaret asked as she dried a plate. Danny had departed as soon as he had arrived, like an airplane dropping a bomb and flying away to safety, oblivious to the destruction in its wake. "Helen?" Margaret turned toward the younger woman.

"What?" Helen jumped, startled at the sound of the older woman's voice. "I'm sorry . . . what did you say?"

Margaret indicated the deputy with a flip of her dish towel and frowned when she saw that he was *still* staring in their direction. "I *said* . . . what's wrong with him? Have you ever known Wan not to sit at the counter?"

"Oh, Margaret . . ." Helen drew her aside to the dividing wall. No one in the dining room could see them as she grabbed her friend's arm and burst into tears.

"Helen . . . sweetheart . . . what in the world?" Margaret

tried to hug the younger woman, but was gently pushed away.

"Margaret, I have done something horrible . . ."

Margaret stood openmouthed as Helen hurriedly dried her tears and peeked around the wall. Mystified, Margaret looked, too, and saw nothing out of the ordinary—save the deputy who was seated in the wrong location with a grim look on his face. "Does this have something to do with your friend . . . the one Danny mentioned?" Helen nodded and looked to the back door. "Helen . . ." Margaret spoke a bit more forcefully this time, hoping to get her attention. It was apparent that the young woman was on the verge of bolting.

Before Margaret could decide what to say, Helen took a deep breath, untied her apron, and handed it to her. "I am sorry to have disappointed you," she said. "You have been good to me . . ."

Margaret was truly at a loss to understand anything that was happening. "Helen," she pleaded, "honey, if you will just tell me what . . ." She made a helpless gesture with her hands as Helen, biting her lip, walked through the door to the dining room.

Wan watched Helen disappear behind the kitchen wall with Margaret. He knew that she had seen him watching her. Wan shook his head. He was getting angrier by the second. *At Helen?* he wondered, endeavoring to organize his thoughts. *No*, he admitted, *I am mostly angry with myself. But wait a minute*, he rationalized, *she is not totally blameless here.*

Wan had no claims on her, he knew that, but she *had* to have known how he felt. *Okay, no claims on her, then what? Hope? Well, yeah*, Wan thought. It was just a punch in the gut to find out she had a guy *living with her* right under his nose. They had been living together! How could she have done this to him?

Wan's mind churned. *Well,* he thought, *they just met, right? So really, they weren't technically living together . . . whew!* Wan felt relieved, much better. *But they were in the same house . . . at night . . . and you know what that means . . .* Wan felt worse, much worse. *The guy did say she gave him the couch.*

"Okay."

Wan looked up. Helen was standing in front of him. Where had she come from? "Excuse me?" he said.

"Okay, what now?"

Wan was confused, and in the present state he had created for himself, it irritated him. "'What now,' what?" he demanded testily.

Helen took a ragged breath. She was trying to maintain her composure. "Can we step outside?" Wan agreed, suddenly aware of all the eyes upon them. Even Margaret, he noticed as he held the door for Helen, was gawking shamelessly from the kitchen, an expression of horror frozen on her face.

Around the corner, Helen turned and said, "Wan, you have always been my friend. I want you to know that this was nothing I planned or even ever imagined."

"You never knew this guy?" Wan said, attempting to keep the suspicion from his voice. "He just . . . appeared?" Helen nodded sadly. "You just invited the guy in? Just 'hey, I don't know who you are, but you're welcome to spend the night'?"

"He was hurt. At the time, I didn't know what else to do."

"Wow. Maybe I should have tried that."

Something began to click inside Helen's head. She was listening carefully to Wan, but somehow it wasn't quite making sense. Her brow furrowed. "I'm sorry?"

"Hey, I never asked for an apology."

"No," Helen said impatiently, still trying to understand, "I don't mean, 'I'm sorry' like 'I'm *sorry*' . . . I mean, 'What are you talking about?' What do you mean 'Wow, I should have tried that'?"

Wan, on course again, took up the offensive. "You invite a guy you don't even know to spend the night, stay awhile . . . a guy is *living with you* because he's hurt? I was just saying, geez, Helen, you won't even go on a *date* with me . . . Hey, I'm not the best-looking guy in the world, and of course, I don't have that romantic English accent, but if I'd known that was what it takes, sheesh, I would have broken *my* arm. I mean, for *that,* a guy gets to spend the night?"

Wan stood with his feet apart. His hands were on his hips, his head cocked and jutted toward Helen at the perfect angle—aggressive, yet cool. He was in complete control, strangely proud of his precise remarks. He was a man for whom the consummate selection of scathing words had just poured from his mouth exactly as he had intended. Crisp and sarcastic, biting and hurtful—words designed to end a conversation the same way a boxer wins a fight, with a triumphant flurry.

That was why Helen's growing smile bewildered him. And with no other option available, Wan stood there, slowly deflating like a bad tire, while the one time in his life he'd just insulted a person to the best of his ability, only to have her hug him around the neck and smile. At that moment, despite the eloquence he had just displayed, Wan was a man like any other, feeling like an idiot in the presence of a beautiful woman—and not knowing why.

As for Helen, under any other circumstance, she would have slapped Wan into next week—perhaps even punched him—for implying what he had. But when it dawned on her what *he* thought was happening (and that she would not be sent to prison), Helen was so relieved that she had to stifle a giggle. And much to Wan's chagrin, she did not stifle it well.

Composing herself but unable to erase altogether her grin, Helen said to the red-faced deputy, "Wan, we will talk about this later. All you need to know is that nothing—listen to me—*nothing* has happened between myself and the gentleman you apparently met at my cottage. Do you understand?"

"Yes," Wan answered meekly.

Helen went back inside, promised Margaret a full explanation to be delivered at a later time, and slipped out the back door to her truck.

Wan, still leaning against the building where Helen had left him, watched her drive away and thought, *Gee. I just figured you were fooling around. And you thought that was funny? Wait 'til you find out I tried to shoot the guy.*

As SHE DROVE, HELEN'S MIND SPUN IN A THOUSAND DIRECTIONS. On the one hand, she was thankful Josef had managed to pull off whatever had happened; on the other, she was mad at him for getting into the situation in the first place. Had Wan said something about "a romantic English accent"? *The accent,* she thought, *that's how he did it.* Helen smiled to herself and shook her head in wonder. *That must've been some awfully fast thinking.*

Suddenly Helen was struck by a thought: *What if he's gone?* She pressed a bit harder on the accelerator. It would only make sense, wouldn't it, for Josef to run? After all, why would he stay? Then another thought struck her, this one more disturbing than the first: *Did she want him to?*

Several days earlier, after Josef had angrily left her on the beach, Helen had not come back to the cottage until dark. It had taken her that long to sort out her thoughts about the loss of Josef's family, his thoughts about forgiveness, the death of her husband, and the possibility that forgiveness might have a place in her life.

When she had entered the cottage that evening, a coolness had existed between the two. Both had been overly polite until Josef had asked if he should leave. "Of course not," Helen had told him. She was so sorry, she had said, about Tatiana and Rosa. Josef had accepted her words gratefully, and soon, they'd begun talking like friends again.

Friends? Are we friends? Helen thought as she bumped down her driveway, craning her neck, looking to see whether Josef was even still there. She pulled to a stop beside the steps. *Unbelievable,* she thought. *I actually want him to be here.*

"Hullo, lady! Odd time of the day for you to be home."

Helen stuck her head out the truck window and looked up. Josef had come out of the cottage and was leaning jauntily against the deck rail, his British persona on full display.

"Hello, Josef," Helen said as she exited the vehicle.

"Might I deduct, from what I confess is your not totally unexpected arrival, that you have recently experienced a conversation with the local constable?"

"You are very perceptive."

"Yes then, well, I would be now, wouldn't I?" Josef

grinned down at Helen and spread his arms. "Genuine fear, it seems, conjures forth a level of consciousness to which I have previously been unaccustomed."

"I'll bet," Helen remarked. "Are you all right?"

Josef exhaled loudly as if to rid himself of his alter ego— the happy Brit—and in his normal voice, he replied, "Yes, I am fine. What about you?"

As Helen began to relate the details of her encounter with Wan at the café, Josef descended the stairs and arranged some old beach furniture under the cottage in the shade. Sitting patiently while she told the story, Josef was relieved (and amazed) to hear that Helen had not really needed to provide any information. They were now free to collaborate on any details it might become necessary to reveal. When she was finished, however, Helen was surprised to see Josef frowning. "What's wrong?" she asked.

"The deputy . . . what was his name? Wan?" Helen nodded. "Wan thought . . . he thought you and I were . . . ahhhh . . . you know?"

"Apparently," she said with an amused smirk.

"Oh, my," Josef said, leaning back hard. "Maybe *that* is why he shot at me."

Helen's head jerked around. "He *shot* at you!" she asked, half standing from her chair, plainly astonished.

"Yes," Josef said, chuckling at her reaction, "and not with a peashooter like the one that got me here." He indicated his shoulder. "The man had a cannon in his hands. It's probably why he missed."

Josef told her the entire tale and asked a few questions of his own. He was particularly interested in Danny and was sorry he'd been frightened. He had only been joking when he intimated the possibility of Wan having shot at him out of jealousy, but insisted to Helen that the idea contained a kernel of truth.

"Wan? And me?" she scoffed. "That's ridiculous."

"To you, maybe yes. To him? Perhaps not so ridiculous."

"But I never . . . I mean, I haven't led him to believe anything of the sort."

Josef made a calming motion with his hands. "I believe you. Sometimes we—by 'we,' I am referring to men in general—sometimes we allow our hopes to obscure reality." Josef was quiet as Helen contemplated that thought. Then he said, "In any case, I believe your deputy to be a good man. Although, luckily for me, a bad shot."

Helen squirmed nervously in the beach chair, trying to take it all in. The day's events so far had proven almost overwhelming.

"*Whatever* your feelings for the deputy," Josef continued, "it is now clear that I must leave. I would have no one think of you what they obviously will when word spreads about a man living at your house—innocent though it may be. Not to mention," he added, "the personal risk you continue to take as you harbor a . . . well, whatever it is that I am." He paused. "I certainly don't *feel* like an enemy of your country . . . though technically, I suppose—"

"Josef," Helen interrupted, "you are not our enemy. At least, you are not *my* enemy."

Helen was somewhat surprised to hear the words coming from her mouth, but her spirit told her they were true. "Listen," she said, the beginnings of an idea formulating in her mind, "maybe you do need to leave here . . ." She gestured with her hands, indicating the cottage. ". . . but it would be crazy—dangerous even—to leave the area."

Josef frowned, not following her reasoning, but she

didn't pause or even slow down. Helen spoke with intensity, leaning toward him, convinced that she was accurate in her assessment of the situation. "Josef . . . the thing with Wan and Danny today was the best thing that could have happened! Look at it this way—number one . . ." She smiled slyly. ". . . Wan will be nice to you. Not in a million years does he want it to become common knowledge that he had a shoot-out with a guy and his rake." Josef laughed. "So," Helen continued, "he'll be subconsciously protecting you. I will guarantee, at this very moment, he is scared to death you might say something. Therefore, he'll be buddy-buddy in public. And so to everyone else . . . 'Hey, he's the deputy's friend.' And that will avert any suspicions anyone might have ordinarily had." Josef began to nod.

"Number two is the fact that someone besides me knows you now. And you *are* the person they met. To Wan and Danny, you are the funny English guy, and that word will spread . . . which brings me to number three.

"We are not living in New York or Washington. Heck, Josef, this isn't even Mobile! This is a small town. And believe me, I know how these people are. They are sweet and kind and proud and protective . . . and before too long, they will be protective of you. You will be *their* funny English guy.

"So, yes, you have to leave here. But, no, you don't have to leave the area. We just have to find another place for you to stay."

And that is how Josef Bartels Landermann, formerly an officer of the Kriegsmarine, came to live in a squatter's cabin tucked quietly away in a pine forest bordering the wild, windswept sand dunes of the Alabama Gulf coast.

Certainly the story could have ended there as well.

Josef's tiny one-room "home" was a bit less than a mile's walk from Helen's cottage. As the summer turned into fall, they visited nearly every evening and talked endlessly about their lives, God, politics, Danny, the war, and whatever else came to mind. They discussed what was important, argued about what was not, and laughed and teased each other about both. They were quiet together and often just sat on the beach, watching the waves, until one or the other of them yawned and said good night.

While Josef still missed Tatiana and Rosa, he no longer dwelled in dark thoughts and was able to look cautiously toward the future. It was, to be sure, a future fraught with uncertainty, but one he no longer faced with fear. Josef had decided to build a new life here in America. After all, wasn't this the country that encouraged new beginnings? A new beginning. A new life. And perhaps . . . he sometimes dared think . . . with a new woman?

As Thanksgiving came and went and Christmas approached, it was apparent that Helen had been correct. After the initial curiosity about the "squatter from England," most of the local community seemed to accept Josef as part of the melting pot America had become. To them, he was just one more fellow, temporarily down on his luck, working his way toward better times.

Josef had discarded his old voice and, with Helen's encouragement, spoke only using his British accent. It seemed safer not to switch back and forth—German to English and vice versa—the odds of being overheard were too great.

Apprehensively at first, Josef had gone into town with

Helen as she ran various errands and was introduced to many of the people there. He became familiar to Billy and Margaret and even did some odd jobs for them at their home and at the café. Mostly electrical work with a bit of carpentry thrown in, it allowed Josef to earn a wage and demonstrate a visible means of support. Undeterred by Helen's protests, he insisted upon paying her back for the expenses she incurred while helping him. Obviously neither of them really knew how much that was, but Helen often found small amounts of cash on her kitchen table that he left during a visit.

Helen was amazed at the relationship developing between Josef and Danny. Somehow, despite their frightening introduction that day at Helen's cottage, the two were becoming fast friends. In addition, when it became apparent that Danny had evidently blocked the most noteworthy part of that day from his memory, Wan also relaxed around Josef.

As far as the deputy was concerned, neither Josef nor Helen had mentioned his mistake, Danny, it seemed, had forgotten it, and *he* certainly wasn't going to bring it up, so . . .

Just as Helen predicted, Wan became Josef's friend and advocate. Though it made her nervous at first, she was gradually getting used to seeing Wan and Josef together.

To Helen's amazement, it was Wan who loaned an old car to Josef—never thinking that his new friend might not have a license to drive. It was also Wan who introduced Josef to the Nelsons and the Callaways—local families with long traditions in fishing and shrimping. Josef learned the trade from them, worked on their boats, and soon was a welcome presence with the other men as they labored together. Most afternoons would find Josef, in line at the fish house with his day's catch, jabbering away in the accent that so amused the crews or listening to the stories of the boat captains as they dumped thousands of pounds of seafood on the conveyors and complained about the scarcity of shrimp and fish. It certainly was better, they assured Josef, in the "old days."

Just as Josef had hoped, his new life was taking shape. Helen was happier, calmer, and beginning to suspect there might be more to her friendship with Josef than she'd allowed herself to imagine. It could have gone on forever. And they had every reason to suspect that it might.

As so often happens, however, even those who do not *expect* the worst find themselves unable to fend it off. And so it was on the morning of Christmas Eve, 1942, during what should have been the most hopeful time of their lives, that Josef and Helen looked up and saw their safe corner of the world altered in the blink of an eye.

CHAPTER 14

WHEN HELEN CAME OUT OF THE COTTAGE, SHE WAS surprised to see Josef standing beside the truck. "Good morning," she said cheerfully. "I thought I was supposed to meet you by the road."

As Helen descended the stairs, Josef gallantly opened the door of the truck for her. "I was up," he said. "I decided to walk. Last chance for a while. Rain is coming." He helped her in, shut the door, and ran around to the other side. Though Josef had Wan's old car, it didn't run well, and he used it only to transport him to the docks and back. Almost every time he went into town, Josef rode with Helen.

"Really?" Helen asked, leaning out the truck's open window and scanning the sky for clouds. "It doesn't look like rain."

"On its way, I assure you. Drop in temperature . . . wind shift. Bad weather on its way."

"Gee," Helen said as she slipped the clutch and gunned the old truck down the driveway, "I hope Santa has his rain jacket!"

The evening before, meeting as usual on the beach, the two had made plans to come into town together for Christmas Eve. Helen had to work only the lunch shift, but wanted to spend some time shopping in Foley before going to work. Shrimping had been slow most of December so Josef had no problem taking a day off—and besides, he was looking forward to spending an entire day with Helen.

They stopped at the café to ask Billy if there was anything he needed from town, and as they parked in front of the small building, Danny came out to say hello. "Merry Christmas, Josef! Merry Christmas, Helen!"

"Merry Christmas to you, Danny," they said in unison.

"My mama has a present for you, Helen, but I don't. I have one for Josef. Here," Danny said as he pulled a small package from his pocket and gave it to Josef. "I made it for you. Open it."

When the paper was torn away, Josef was speechless. He held the item up for Helen to see. "Oh, Danny," she gasped. "You made this?" He nodded proudly.

It was an intricate carving, about the size of a man's finger, of a speckled trout. Its proportion was flawless, the detail incredible. Josef was stunned. "Danny . . . I don't know what to say. Thank you. It's beautiful. I didn't know you could do this."

"I didn't know I could do it, either," Danny said. "It's my first one. I did it with my daddy's pocketknife. Are you coming inside? My mama saw you drive up and said if you are going to town, could you get a sack of flour and a tin of lard from the store? She said you would know what kind to get. Are you coming inside?"

"Well, Danny," Helen said as Josef waved at Margaret through the front window, "I don't have to come inside now. You've taken care of all the details for me. But I'll be back in a couple of hours." Then she wiggled her eyebrows at Danny and added, "We have some errands to run for Santa Claus!"

"Okay! Okay!" Danny rubbed his hands together excitedly. "I'm gonna tell my daddy!" Before he went back into the café, however, Danny wrapped Josef in a big bear hug. "I love you, Josef. Merry Christmas again. Merry Christmas again to you, too, Helen. I will make a present for you next year."

As they watched the young man make his way back inside, Helen shook her head in wonder and took the carved trout from Josef, examining it again. "I love you, Josef," she murmured softly, repeating the words that had come from Danny, surprising them both only moments before. She handed the carving back. Looking carefully at the man before her, Helen asked, "Why does he love you, Josef?"

Josef didn't know how to answer the question and sat silently, a bit uncomfortable, unsure about that himself. Helen answered for him. "Because you possess a good and true spirit," she explained. "Danny senses that you are not concerned about what he is . . . only about what he can become. Danny does not process shades of gray. He sees life only in black and white. In a way he could never define, he perceives you to be worthy of his love. I believe that too."

Josef was still, held prisoner by Helen's gaze. After her words had been spoken, the silent seconds that followed seemed to last an eternity. Neither moved. Josef wanted to take her in his arms, to hold this woman, to kiss her. Helen thought he might. Instead, the words that came out of *his* mouth were, "I think I'll get him a pocketknife."

Helen's eyebrows raised. "What?" she said.

"I . . . Ahhh . . . I would like to get Danny a pocketknife. He said he used Billy's to carve the fish. And it is beautiful, certainly, just like it is, but he should have his own. Knife. He should have his own knife. And I can get one *for* him."

Josef was babbling and knew it, but he couldn't find an exit line. Helen found it for him.

"Josef," she said, placing her hand on his arm, "let's go get one."

Her touch flustered Josef, and it showed. He looked at Helen as if he had no idea what she was talking about, and she struggled to keep from smiling. "Josef. Let's go get a knife for Danny."

Josef blinked. "Yes," he said. "Yes, let's do."

Crosby's Drugs on Laurel Avenue was decorated with large multicolored lights. Reds, blues, greens—it was the only business in Foley that had been able to obtain these modern bulbs, and the effect was startling. It was as beautiful as anything in New York, everyone agreed. Roy Musso, the pharmacist who wore a Santa hat, added to the atmosphere. Crosby's Drugs epitomized Christmas to the local people, and the threat of rain or the fact that there had never, ever been the slightest possibility of snow—even though the temperature *had* dropped all the way to fifty-six degrees—dampened their enthusiasm not one bit.

On the second shelf next to the Little Orphan Annie Official Decoder Rings, there were several pocketknives from which to choose. Josef settled on a dark bone-handled Schrade that had two blades. At sixty cents, it was expensive, but Josef had the money and was determined that Danny should have a knife equal to his obvious talent.

As they waited for the gift to be wrapped, Josef smiled mysteriously and asked, "Would it be possible to separate for a bit? I have some shopping I would like to accomplish on my own, if you don't mind."

Helen feigned a display of innocent confusion. "Why can't I go with you?" she teased. "Aren't we having fun?"

Josef lifted his chin and looked away to demonstrate the fact that he was unmoved by her plea. "Sorry," he said. "What did you tell Danny? I am on an errand for Santa Claus!"

Helen laughed, but as she noticed a sudden change in Josef's expression, her laughter died away. Josef had turned his head toward the drugstore's big picture window while talking with Helen, but was now staring intently through it at something that had captured his undivided attention. "Josef," she said, suddenly concerned, "what is it? What's wrong?" She tried to follow his gaze.

"Who is that man?" he asked. Josef had an uneasy feeling, but could not place the figure huddled inside the cab of a heavily loaded flatbed truck. He was familiar somehow. Too familiar.

"What man?" Helen asked, straining to see. "Where?"

"The black truck with the cargo boxes . . . across the street."

Helen focused now and saw an old man. He was dirty—she could see that from where she was standing. He wore a baseball cap, had a long gray beard, and apparently was parked, just sitting there, doing nothing. "I know who that is," Helen said, involuntarily curling her lip. "He's only been in the café a couple of times, and Billy waits on him. He won't let any of us do it. Billy can't stand him."

"Do you know his name?"

"Kramer. It's 'something' Kramer. I've heard Wan and the others talk about him too. They don't like him at all."

Josef had not moved. "What does he do?"

Helen shrugged. "Ahhhh . . . fishing? I think?"

"Does he have a boat with a red top?"

"Josef, I don't know. You're scaring me," Helen said. "What is this about? Why do *you* recognize him?"

Josef exhaled. His mind was already working furiously when he answered. "Because," he said, "he has a boat with a red top."

Moving quickly, Josef swept the gift-wrapped package from the counter and took Helen's arm. "We must leave *now*," he said. "Hurry. This man must not see me."

Walking fast to keep up as they moved toward the door, Helen was frightened. "Josef," she said, "what's this about? Who is he to you?"

"Let's get out of here and I'll tell you later," he answered.

The truck was parked less than twenty feet from the drugstore's front door. It would be a simple matter, Josef knew, to cover his face with a hand as if to shield his eyes or straighten his hair and step quickly to the vehicle. They would be away in seconds. Kramer wasn't even looking in their direction.

Helen was close behind Josef as he ducked his head, threw a hand to his brow, and powered through the door. She bumped him when he stopped. Looking around Josef, Helen could see that he had literally run into a man who was entering the store. The man had come around the corner beside the entrance and simply gotten caught in their stampede.

Helen placed her hand on Josef's back, preparing to continue on out the door, but Josef didn't move. Helen pushed gently and maneuvered to the side a bit in an effort to see Josef's face. No one had said, "Excuse me," or "I'm sorry." In fact, neither man had moved at all.

"Josef?" she said hesitantly. But Josef did not respond. He was not being rude or inattentive. In his defense, Josef had never even heard Helen's voice. Josef's focus at that moment was narrowed to a pinpoint as his heart hammered in his ears. It was the sound of his life being torn apart, but still, he did not move. He was frozen by the face of the man in front of him . . . the face of Ernst Schneider.

AS THE BLUE CHEVY TRUCK, ALREADY POINTED TOWARD THE south, screeched away in that direction, Schneider ran across the street. "Go," he said, leaping into the flatbed cab and slamming the door behind him. "Go! Follow them!"

"Calm down," Kramer said as he made a slow U-turn across the middle of the street. "I saw you over there. I saw them two run. Won't do 'em no good."

"What do you mean?" Schneider demanded. "And hurry up! Let's go!"

"Hey, boy!" Kramer growled as he suddenly lifted his foot from the accelerator, slowing the truck even more. "You don't talk to me that way. You do . . . we gon' have problems. I *ain't* hurrying up 'cause I know where to find 'em. And I *ain't* hurrying up 'cause you ain't gon' do nothin' to 'em with me around. I ain't gon' be a part of moppin' up your messes."

Ernst Schneider seethed, but he said nothing. He had only two weeks left in the miserable place anyway, and he was too smart by far to be lured into a confrontation with an imbecile like Harris Kramer. In a way, however, Schneider identified with the man. *You do not talk to me that way, either,* he said silently to the filthy man driving the truck. *You are correct. We will have problems.*

Schneider planned to kill Kramer anyway before he left. *Only two more weeks,* he mused. *Almost finished. And now this.* Schneider shook his head as he saw Josef's face in his mind's eye. *How could this have happened?*

Last July, Schneider's coded message aboard the U-166

had ordered him ashore. There he was to use a crystal set—
a radio—that had already been constructed in the attic of a
fish house to contact and direct U-boats toward any merchant ships or troop transports departing Mobile Bay.
Further, he was to direct fire on any vessel of *any* kind moving east or west, into or out of the Mississippi River basin.
Transportation ashore, he was informed, would be provided
by a man already in place—the owner of the fish house.

Aware that his departure was imminent, Schneider
devised a plan that would allow him to embarrass
Commander Kuhlmann, enrich himself, and exact the ultimate revenge from the swine Landermann.

That night, as Kramer's boat had come into view,
Schneider put his scheme into motion. Kuhlmann, thinking
only that the U-166 was to receive a delivery of some sort,
had gone below to retrieve gold from the safe. The possibility that Schneider was *leaving* had not entered his mind.
While the commander was below, Schneider had taken the
opportunity to shoot Josef and was waiting casually on deck
when Kuhlmann returned.

"Where's Landermann?" he had asked, upon finding
Schneider alone.

The Nazi indicated the red-topped vessel tied by only one
line and answered that the cadet, Landermann, had gone on
board to unload a specific piece of cargo. After only a short
time, Schneider expressed his impatience by wondering aloud
about the delay. Declaring his intention to "find out what
was taking so long," he prepared to board Kramer's vessel.
Before he stepped onto the boat, however, he paused as if a
thought had just occurred to him. "Give me the gold," he
had suggested to Kuhlmann. "I will settle our finances while
I am on board. After all," he had remarked to the com-

mander, "who trusts a spy? No matter *what* side he is on."

Kuhlmann agreed that it was probably prudent not to allow a "spy" aboard the submarine at all and handed the gold over to Schneider. "I will strike a hard bargain for the Führer," the Nazi had said as he stepped to the rail, "and will return with the gold that is not required."

Those had been the last words Schneider had spoken to Kuhlmann, who, in accordance with established procedure that required an officer on deck when docked with another vessel, stayed behind.

Schneider disappeared into the boat momentarily, then reappeared as the boat's engines unexpectedly roared to life. Then, to Kuhlmann's utter astonishment, Schneider released the line from the red-topped boat and waved. "Landermann and I will be back shortly," he had shouted.

Commander Kuhlmann, totally taken in by the ruse, had waited, his unease and suspicions building by the hour, until dawn, when he was forced by the submarine's close proximity to shore to submerge and sail away. He believed that, most likely, something tragic had befallen the Nazi observer and Josef, his friend, but he was never able to fully grasp just what that might have been.

It should have been perfect, Schneider thought as he rode silently in the flatbed truck, second-guessing every move he'd made that night in July. Every single piece of his plan that night had come together. Or so he had assumed. It was disappointing, he admitted to himself, to find that Landermann, in such a minor role, had not even been capable of playing his part. It had been a grand production, but now it was ruined. Schneider grimaced as he thought about Josef. *You were supposed to die, fool!*

Working to control his fury, Schneider cut his eyes to the

side and glanced at Kramer. The man was driving as if he hadn't a care in the world. The Nazi silently cursed. While he had expected an elite practitioner of espionage as his partner and guide when he came ashore, he had instead been saddled with this buffoon—an obnoxious, lazy, infuriating piece of filth if ever there had been one.

Kramer spoke. "That was the boy you shot on the sub, weren't it." His words were phrased as a statement, not as a question. Schneider did not respond. The old man cackled gleefully. "Yeah, I thought so." He laughed again. "Missed 'im, didn't you? I thought so that night. You's too wrapped up in what you's sayin' to actually *aim!*"

Laughing uproariously and warming to the subject, Kramer continued to needle Schneider, whose level of rage was rising dangerously. "Look here, son . . . you gonna kill a man, you just kill 'im. You take your *time* with a woman, but you get a man done. You ain't careful, he'll bite you back. I done both. I know. Unh-huh . . . man, you get him dead quick."

Kramer wasn't even attempting eye contact with Schneider. He had lost himself in a favorite subject and continued to chatter away. "You winged 'im. I'd a told you it wadn't no full-on hit that night. I saw the boy hanging on one'a my boat tires." Kramer smiled broadly. "Yessir, coulda plucked 'im right outta the water and finished 'im proper. Would have too. But you . . ." The old man looked over at Schneider, expressing an air of superior intelligence. "Naww! You come on *my* boat all high and mighty—the Führer this and the Führer that . . . turning your nose up at me? Bossing *me* around?"

Schneider fumed silently. Was it really necessary to endure this? Wasn't it enough that he'd lived in the attic of a fish house, eating the garbage this cretin prepared? That for months now, he had been without proper companionship and breathing the foul air of this sick society?

Schneider was about half a beat from back-handing the old man, and Kramer must have sensed it. He said, "You be nice, boy. You be nice to old Harris. You wanna finish what you started? You wanna get that boy? Put 'im down? I can put you on 'im. I know where the girl works."

Kramer drove past the café and only glanced to see if Helen's truck was there. It wasn't. He didn't want to reveal to Schneider the young woman's place of employment just yet. *Get this psycho back to the fish house,* he thought. *I'll tell him then. I'll be out of it.*

Kramer was nothing if not an expert in the art of self-preservation. He harbored no illusions about what would happen to the man Schneider was after . . . or the girl if she didn't cooperate. Or Schneider himself if he wasn't careful. Harris Kramer had killed before—four times to be exact—but they were smart killings, all for cash, not done in the heat of the moment.

Kramer was glad Schneider would soon be leaving. It had been too much trouble and not enough money. That's why he'd done it, of course. For the money. After all, Harris Kramer didn't like the Germans. In fact, he hated them. Just like he hated everybody else.

By the time the flatbed truck had pulled up in front of the fish house, Kramer had told Schneider where Helen worked and laid out a plan. "Steal a car so you can dump it later," he said. "Grab the girl. It don't even matter if they see ya—they don't know where you come from. You only been in town twice, and you're leaving soon anyway. So grab the girl and make her take you to the guy."

Schneider had agreed that it was a workable proposal and determined that it was what he would do. Kramer refused to drive him away from the fish house, but pointed him down the road. Walk, he'd told him. There was a group of houses near Navy Cove. It was no more than a mile, Kramer had said. "Get yourself a car there. Them idiots leave their keys in 'em. Just walk in and take one."

Schneider set out to do just that. He had walked almost a hundred yards from the fish house when Harris Kramer hailed him at the top of his voice. "Hey, boy!" Schneider turned to look. "Merry Christmas!" he screamed, dissolving into a demented fit of laughter.

CAREENING DOWN HIGHWAY 3, HELEN HAD LISTENED AS JOSEF had filled in the blanks for her. He had told her some time back about Schneider and the events leading up to her having found him washed ashore. Now, unfortunately, Helen had a face to go with the name.

She had insisted Josef leave her at the café. "Billy's here. I'll be fine," she had said. "Just take the truck and go. Leave it at my cottage or in the woods—whatever—but *you* get to your cabin. It's hidden. No one knows where it is, and it can't be reached by car."

It appeared to both Josef and Helen that they had gotten away—at least from the flatbed truck—and that the immediate danger had passed. They were relieved that there was now time to regroup, to plan, and to consider their next move.

After expressing her remorse to Margaret and Billy for forgetting to buy the supplies they had asked for, Helen nervously went about her work. Margaret had noticed the frantic conversation between Helen and Josef when they had driven up. She had also seen the gravel fly as Josef spun the truck away from the café and continued south. By the time Helen walked through the door, Margaret had already remarked to Billy that "something was up." After accepting the young woman's apology and assuring her that she needed to do some final Christmas shopping anyway, Margaret got the keys to their vehicle from Billy and went to Foley herself.

It was not yet lunchtime, and the café dining room was empty. Danny was in and out every five minutes reporting to Billy about the storm clouds, asking when it would rain, and concerned about whether Santa could fly in it if it did. Billy was keeping a keen eye on Helen, who appeared to be on the verge of bolting. Not that she could have gone anywhere had she wanted to. Josef had her truck, and Margaret had theirs.

Billy was in the kitchen and had begun folding dough for the lunch biscuits when Helen cried out. Jerking around, Billy quickly looked through the kitchen's order window and saw Helen stumble as she backed frantically toward the counter.

Schneider had executed the initial part of his impromptu plan in an orderly manner. He had taken the first car he'd come upon near the group of houses at Navy Cove—a black Ford sedan. Kramer had been correct; the keys were in it. Schneider drove east until he'd come to Highway 3, turned north, and was soon pulling into the parking lot of the café.

Schneider saw the young woman through the front window only seconds before she saw him. He leaped cursing from the car. He'd hoped to be able to take her quietly— maybe show her the pistol hidden in his pocket and compel her to leave without any trouble. *Not possible now,* he thought. Schneider could see her scrambling backward, bumping past tables in the dining room as he ran to the front door. *Do this quickly,* Schneider commanded himself as he burst inside.

Danny was behind the register. He stood, confused and frightened by Helen's reaction to the man who had just exploded through the entrance. Billy was out of the kitchen in an instant and rounded the counter. He, too, saw the man coming for Helen and was moving quickly to head him off. It was Billy's intention to get between them. "Hang on here!" Billy roared. "What the heck do you—" Billy drew up short when the man shoved a gun in his face.

"Move back, old man," Schneider snarled, "or die right now."

Billy's mouth fell open. He looked at Helen. "Don't, Billy," she warned, never taking her eyes off Schneider, who had shifted the pistol into his other hand and was maneuvering around Billy toward her. "Don't do anything. He wants Josef."

"Why?" Billy asked her. Then to Schneider, "Who are you?"

"Shut up! Shut up!" Schneider yelled, threatening Billy with the pistol again. Watching the older man closely, the Nazi reached out and grabbed Helen's arm, his grip causing her to cry out in pain.

From behind Schneider came a voice from someone he had not seen upon entering the café. Danny had tears running down his face, and though he was as scared as he had ever been, the young man was coming to the rescue of his father and his friend. "You let her go," Danny said, "and you stop scaring my daddy. You are bad! I will hurt you!"

"Danny, no!" Helen and Billy spoke almost as one.

"Go back, Danny," Billy said. "It's all right."

At first, Schneider thought he had been trapped. Hearing the voice behind him, he had almost dropped the gun, but now . . . what was this? Schneider turned. When he saw Danny, his eyes opened wide, he grinned, then laughed out loud. "Don't you laugh at me," Danny said, crying harder.

Schneider cocked his head and directed his attention to Billy. Continuing to hold Helen by the arm, he gestured toward Danny with the gun. "Does this *thing* belong to you?"

Billy's face darkened. He had never felt so helpless in his life. For all his bluster, Billy was a patient and loving man. There had been people in his life he hadn't liked—even some he had avoided altogether—but until this moment, Billy had never truly and completely hated another person. In a momentary wisp of realization that swirled through his consciousness, Billy *knew* that he was looking into the face of evil, and he was acutely aware that had he possessed the means and opportunity to kill this man, he would have done so without hesitation.

"Maybe you did not hear me," Schneider said. "This thing here . . . does this dummy belong to you?"

"Don't you dare say that about him," Helen hissed.

Schneider looked surprised. "What's this? You have feelings for the dummy?" He leaned toward Danny, who was sobbing quietly, and pointed the gun between his eyes. "I think we will shoot him . . . Watch this."

"Oh, God, please," Billy breathed, his knees buckling.

"No! No! No!" Helen screamed, struggling violently.

Schneider managed to hold on to her, but Helen's hysterics had forced him to lower the gun. Danny, crying again, was looking at Billy and whispering, "Daddy? Daddy?"

Schneider laughed at him again, once more raising the gun. "You are an inferior," he said disgustedly.

"Stop!" Helen pleaded. Then, convinced Schneider was really about to shoot, she said, "If you do this, I swear, you'll never find Josef. I'll never tell you where he is."

The Nazi stopped and appeared to contemplate her threat. "And if I don't," he said, offering Helen a nasty alternative, "if I *don't* shoot him, you *will* take me to Josef?"

Helen thought only for a moment. It was their fault—Josef's and hers—that Billy and Danny were being threatened in this way. She had to get this madman away from them. There was no other choice. "Yes," she said.

It had begun to rain. Schneider had forced Helen to drive, and as she did, she struggled to think of a way out of this nightmare. Or at least a way to somehow warn Josef before he was murdered. Yet, she berated herself, to save her life, she could not produce an idea with greater sophistication than shouting a warning when they got close to Josef's cabin. *To save my life,* Helen thought and almost laughed aloud at the irony.

Helen was horrified. She was taking this man directly to where Josef was hiding . . . and doing so without resistance or deceit. Schneider had impressed upon her that if she did *not*, he'd take her back to the café and make her watch him kill Danny in front of his father. She believed the man and, therefore, was doing as he ordered.

"Why are you stopping here?" Schneider asked, suddenly suspicious as Helen pulled the car off the road, seemingly in the middle of nowhere.

"His place—the cabin Josef lives in—is through the

woods in that direction about a quarter to a half mile."
Helen pointed. "There's a pathway, but no road."

Schneider hesitated briefly, but detected no guile in the
young woman. "Pull the car down the pathway so that it
can't be seen."

"But the sand—"

"Just do as I say."

She did. Helen backed the car up and headed it through
the brush that bordered the road. As the car slowed, binding
in the soft, wet ground, she didn't use the clutch, allowing it
to stall, then lose power completely. "Told you," she said
with a bit too much satisfaction in her voice for Schneider's
taste. The vehicle remained in sight of the road, which was
her intention, and he knew it.

Though restricted somewhat by the close confines of
the automobile's interior, Schneider reached across and
slapped Helen as hard as he could. "That will be your only
warning," he said calmly and rather proud of his emotional control, considering what she'd just done. "Get out
of the car."

Helen was stunned—literally and figuratively—and truly
frightened of this man. As she staggered from the car, Helen
wiped at her nose and saw that she was bleeding. With every
passing moment, she was becoming less confident that she
could somehow outsmart Schneider. It was obvious that she
could not hope to overpower him.

"This way?" Schneider asked with a gesture as he drew
the gun from his jacket. Helen nodded and watched as the
Nazi checked the semiautomatic's chamber to make certain
it was ready to fire. Helen had no way of knowing, but it
was the same pistol—the Walther PPK—Schneider had used
on Josef the first time. *Now,* Schneider thought, absently

brushing raindrops from the weapon that reappeared immediately, *to finish the job.*

Before Schneider started toward the cabin, he had a
word of warning for Helen. "Listen to me carefully," he
said. "You will walk directly to the cabin that you have indicated is less than a half mile away. You will do so slowly and
in silence. You will inform me *quietly* when we are within
two hundred yards of Landermann's location. You will not
attempt to call out or signal Landermann in any way until I
order you to do so."

As he spoke to the wet, bleeding young woman,
Schneider probed Helen's eyes with his own. Searching for
any sign of treachery, he saw none, but he was determined
that, this time, he would leave nothing to chance. "To be fair,
I must inform you . . . should you ignore these instructions
. . . should you defy me in any way . . . I will kill you immediately. And not with the swift grace of a bullet in the head.
I will break your neck." Then, smiling as if he had finished
placing an order at a fine restaurant, he said, "Excellent. Do
we understand each other?" The smile vanished. "Move."

Helen picked her way through the scrub pines and palmettos. Still attempting to give Josef *some* warning that they
were coming, she had chosen to ignore the small pathway
Josef had worn from the cabin to the road. *Get off it just a
bit,* she told herself. *This maniac won't notice, and maybe
Josef will hear us if we push through this brush.*

But Josef did *not* hear them approach. Coming in sheets
now, the rain was absent the thunder and lightning that
often accompanied even winter storms on the Gulf coast,
but pushed by a strong north wind, the heavy drops pounding the palmetto fronds provided all the cover for which
Schneider could have hoped.

Helen stopped and indicated to the Nazi that their location was now within shouting distance of the cabin. In fact, she pointed out to him, there it was, through the trees. With smoke pouring from the makeshift chimney—actually a piece of metal pipe that had been fitted through the cabin's patchwork roof—the structure was easily visible. Helen had taken Schneider as close as she dared before stopping, again in hopes that Josef would be warned, but it had not worked.

As she waited for Schneider to make his next move—he was examining the situation warily—Helen was aware of an aura of sadness enveloping her like a shroud. This man had outmaneuvered or overpowered them at almost every turn. She began to cry and was conscious of her tears as they silently mingled with the raindrops on her face and fell to the ground, evanescing into nothingness. *An apt metaphor for the happiness in my life,* Helen mused grimly. *An apt metaphor for my life. Always fading into nothingness. And now, for the last time . . .*

Suddenly Helen knew what she would do. A final statement of sorts. She would not live through it, of course, but maybe she could save Josef. She would run. Right now, she would run! Schneider would shoot her. Of that, Helen was certain, but the sound of the shot would warn Josef and give him the time and opportunity to slip away. She took a deep breath, ready to break and run. *Go!* she commanded herself, but inconceivably she was thwarted again before she could move.

Schneider ran his hand roughly up the back of Helen's neck into her wet hair. His fingers spread wide apart, he grabbed as much of it as he could, then gave his hand a full twist. The pain was excruciating, but the humiliation was complete. He had done it again. The Nazi had anticipated her every effort and blocked any attempt to help, to warn, to escape, even to die.

With the pistol in one hand and Helen, quite literally, in the other, Schneider advanced on the cabin. "Mr. Landermann!" he called out weirdly. "Come out and play, Mr. Landermann! Come see what I have for you!"

Helen kicked at him and struggled. She was mad and hurting and panicked by this man who was clearly insane, but she could not free herself from his grip. Irritated by her violent movement, Schneider merely shook Helen like a rat and continued walking.

"Landermann! Mr. Landermann!" Schneider was *singing* Josef's name now. Helen was about to pass out . . . when he halted.

Josef *had* been inside the cabin—a structure with a roof of mostly tin—and because of the rain beating down had not heard Schneider wailing his name until he was fairly close. He had known who it was. With only one entrance—not counting a window that was too small to even wiggle through—Josef saw no chance of subterfuge or any kind of a sneak attack. Choosing what he saw as his only option, Josef poured out of the cabin ready to fight. What he saw when he got outside, however, stopped him in his tracks.

The sight of Helen—bleeding, wet, and being brutally mistreated—drained every ounce of aggression from Josef. He had seen instantly that Schneider held a gun to her head and therefore, acquiesced immediately. "Was soll ich tun?" Josef asked. *What do you want me to do?*

"Ahhh . . ." Schneider showed surprise and responded in German, "In der sprache des Vaterlands. Zuruck. Zuruck in die hutte." *In the tongue of the Fatherland, I see. Back up. Back into the shack.*

Josef did as he asked. Schneider advanced with Helen still in his grip. When they entered the cabin, the Nazi sent Josef to the other side of the room and carefully closed the door behind him. "Was jetzt?" Josef asked sharply. *What now?* He continued to speak in German, thinking that maybe, if Helen did not understand whatever Schneider might say about why he was here or his whereabouts, perhaps she would be spared.

Schneider was about to kill *him*. Of that, he had no doubt whatsoever. The only thing that kept Josef from rushing the Nazi was Helen. He would rather Schneider coolly cut him down than risk enraging the man and have him shoot Helen out of spite. Schneider threw Helen toward Josef, who caught her and put his arms around her.

Schneider pointed the gun at Josef, who gently moved Helen away. "I have always hated you, Landermann," the Nazi said. He spoke loudly, making himself heard above the sound of the rain upon the roof. Brightening, he added, "But you know that, don't you? I believe it was the theme—if not the exact words—of my address to you our last evening aboard the U-166."

Helen knew Josef was being threatened, but was confused by the German. She didn't understand a word. "What is he saying?" she asked Josef. "Why are you—" Josef put out a hand to quiet her.

Schneider continued, "Here is a very curious thing, Landermann. You are now about to be shot by the same man for a second reason." He grinned broadly. "The first time, to be honest, I shot you only because I wanted to. Now, however, I must. I think you will agree, that does take some of the fun out of it . . . turns a . . . oh, how can I explain this? . . . It turns a recreational killing into more of a business event, a duty." Schneider made a show of flicking the safety off the Walther. "So let's get this over with, shall we?" He smiled and gestured toward Helen with his free hand. "I should like to get rid of *you* in order to have some time alone with *her* before *she* dies."

An expression of horror clouded Josef's face, and Schneider laughed at him. Josef knew nothing else to do at that point, but beg. It was his last hope. He would beg for Helen's life. "Ernst, please . . ."

Schneider's eyebrows lifted. "Ernst, is it now?" he said. "My, my . . . *Josef* . . . what?"

"Sir, please . . . I am begging you . . . please do not harm this woman."

Schneider shook the pistol loosely at Josef. "Wait, wait," he said as if he were impatient, which, of course, he was not. Actually Schneider was enjoying himself immensely. "You need to say that part again . . . that last thing, about begging . . . and 'please do not harm this woman,' but say it in English, *Josef*. I think she would like to hear this."

Josef repeated himself. "Please . . . I am begging you . . ."

"You said, 'Sir . . . please . . .' Go back to the beginning."

Josef's head was swimming. Schneider was laughing at him, taunting. Still, if he could persuade him to spare Helen, well, Josef would do anything. "Sir, please, I am begging you. Please do not harm this woman."

"Excellent!" Schneider said to Josef. Addressing Helen, he asked, "Wasn't that beautiful?" Back to Josef. "I must have a reason. So, give me a reason. Why should I spare her?" The Nazi spread his feet apart and placed both hands on the pistol. Aiming it more threateningly at Josef, he said, "Tell me, quickly."

Josef spoke as calmly as he could, "Because I am in love with her."

Schneider's mouth opened in exaggerated surprise, and he lowered the gun. "Really? That is absolutely wonderful! You are in *love* with her. Oh, my. That settles it then. For you, Josef, my friend . . . I will kill her first!"

Schneider did not wait for Josef's reaction. He merely raised the pistol and aimed carefully at Helen, who was standing only six feet away. To Josef, it seemed as if everything were slowing down. He registered the evil grin on Schneider's face, saw Helen flinch as the Nazi's finger tightened on the trigger, and gathered himself desperately to leap in front of Helen, the woman he loved.

But he was too late. Already in the air, Josef closed his eyes in anguish as the roar of the shot filled the tiny cabin. He fell to the floor, face-first, and lay there screaming his grief and rage, waiting for—wanting—the bullet that would next be his.

CHAPTER 15

JOSEF FELT THE GUN TOUCH THE BACK OF HIS HEAD AND stiffened. *Go ahead,* he thought. *Do it.*

"Get up, Josef."

He turned and saw Helen. At first, he couldn't move, so close was he to passing out. Then Josef crawled to her, vaguely aware that the gun was aimed at him now . . . and tracking every move he made. But at this moment, he didn't care. Not at all. "Helen. Helen," Josef said again and again as he took her hand in both of his, kissed it, and wept uncontrollably. "Oh, my God! I don't believe it."

"Josef. Get up now."

Josef stopped crying and steeled himself for what was to come. He breathed deeply in order to control his sobs, kissed Helen's hand a final time, and stood.

The gun was in his face. Josef looked into the barrel and closed his eyes. In a way, he had always known this would happen. It was over.

"Talk quick. Who *are* you?"

"I can explain everything."

"I'm sure you can," Wan said. "But at the moment, Helen, I ain't talking to you. I'm talking to him." Never taking his shotgun from his shoulder, the deputy said, "One more time, Josef . . . make that one *last* time . . . who are you?"

And so Josef laid out the story from the beginning. He told Wan how he'd been surprised and shot that night on the submarine, how he had been nursed back to health by Helen, and how he had decided to stay in America. Josef was completely honest. He left nothing out.

With Helen to prompt him, he gave Wan every piece of information he could remember about Ernst Schneider, from their early confrontations at Oxford to this very moment, allowing the deputy to come to his own conclusions about how the Nazi had ended up here, on the floor of a squatter's cabin in Alabama, ripped to bloody shreds by the double-aught buckshot Wan had fired from his Winchester pump.

BILLY'S CAFÉ HAD BEEN ONE OF THE FIRST LOCATIONS TO INSTALL a telephone. Ward Snook, who had come to the Gulf coast from Ohio in 1908, maintained two lines known as Gulf Telephone Company. One ran from Foley to the state park headquarters the governor had established in Gulf Shores; the other was a party line serving eighteen customers, of which the Hungry Mullet Café was one.

The telephone itself was an eyesore. It was a big, ugly wooden box hanging on the wall with a mouthpiece and a hand crank by which you reached an operator, who would then connect your call. In theory anyway. Mary Nell Brindley, lead operator, seemed most nights to be in the bathroom as much as she was on the switchboard. Sometimes a caller would reach her . . . sometimes not. Even if you did, Margaret noted on more than one occasion, like as not, there was already someone on the line.

Billy had not particularly wanted the telephone, but Ward Snook was a frequent patron of the café and had always been nice to Danny, so Billy had it put in as soon as it had become available. After John Lewis, who owned the Ford dealership in Foley, Billy had been the second businessman to participate in the party line. "Always available in an emergency," Billy said to someone or another almost every day. After all, many people had never seen a telephone "in person," and it was an obvious topic of conversation. And always available in an emergency. Always . . . except today.

As soon as Schneider left the café with Helen in tow, Billy ran to the telephone. He didn't even pause to calm Danny, who was frantic—frightened out of his wits and on the brink of hysteria because Helen had been taken. Billy cranked the telephone furiously over and over again, finally almost tearing it off the wall when he hit it with his fist. "Dead as a hammer!" he yelled to no one in particular, but then, to Danny, said, "Come on, Son. We got to go."

Billy didn't have any idea about what to do except try to hitch a ride to Foley and the sheriff's department. He didn't have his truck, the telephone didn't work, no one else was there . . . Billy and Danny half ran, half walked up Highway 3 in the pouring rain for several minutes, but saw no one, which was not unusual at all for that time of day on that stretch of Highway 3.

Then, early for lunch, also not unusual, Wan appeared, headed south right toward them. Billy and Danny flagged the deputy down and piled into the squad car, telling their tale as fast as they could and urging him to use all the speed he had. Wan dropped them back at the café, but in the two minutes Billy and Danny spent with Wan, they told him everything he needed to know. Only seconds later, Wan was dashing toward the beach, lights flashing, siren wailing.

Helen's cottage first, Wan thought, mustering all his senses to attention. He had to think this situation through as clearly as he could and, at the same time, avoid wrecking the squad car as the rain pelted his windshield and threatened to spin the speeding vehicle into a ditch. *I don't think they'll be there, but I can check quickly. If I miss 'em and have to go back . . .* Wan did not want to consider the consequences. *Well . . . I just can't miss 'em.*

The deputy was trying to remember everything Billy said. The older man was in shock, and Danny appeared well beyond that. *Billy said the guy had some kind of an accent. Midwest, he thought maybe? Somewhere up north? And he wanted Josef.* That made no sense. *For what?* Wan threw possibilities around in his mind for a bit, but got no closer to an answer. *You want a poor British guy bad enough to come in a place waving a gun around? Why? What for?* Not that it really mattered to Wan. The way he saw it, only two things were important about this call. One, the guy obviously had a gun. Two, he had Helen.

Before he made it to the entrance of Helen's driveway, Wan recalled that Billy said they were in a black Ford. "Sedan?" the deputy asked.

"Yes," Billy answered. That saved him some time, Wan knew. No sedan was *ever* making it down Helen's driveway. Not through that sand. Which meant that if this guy—whoever he was—had Helen at *her* cottage, the car would be visible from the road.

It wasn't. Wan hit the gas and sped on by.

Less than a minute later, he spotted the car, abandoned

just off the road. *Alabama plates. Baldwin County,* he noted. *Stolen. Billy'd have known the guy if he was local.*

The vehicle looked as if it had been driven off the road and stuck in the sand on purpose. *Not a very good job of hiding it,* Wan thought as he looked around cautiously. *Some kind of signal? If Helen was driving, yes. Good girl. You're telling me where you are.*

Wan knew the squatter's cabin Josef was living in, though he had never visited the Englishman there. Even before the deputy had helped Josef get a car for his own use, Wan, who occasionally gave Josef a lift, always met him at the road. Nonetheless, Wan had been to the actual cabin several times before Josef ever arrived in the area. They were official visits—sheriff's business—for one reason or another, one family or another. Wan knew his way around in these woods.

Before Deputy Wan Cooper left the squad car, he grabbed up the twelve-gauge Winchester pump. Rarely used, the shotgun's barrel had been shortened a bit and was held in a clamp under the front seat. The gun's magazine had been unplugged and therefore held four shells instead of two. The chamber was empty, which it always was until the gun was needed.

The rain, now whipping through the pines, was a mixed blessing. *I can't hear anything,* Wan thought. *But then, neither can they.* The deputy knew the sounds of the rain and wind would mask his approach. Still, he decided, it was better to make any noise he had to make before he got too close. Working the action on the short-barreled pump, Wan jacked a shell into the chamber.

He hurried through the brush, having declined to advance down the center of the normal pathway. Wan arrived at the cabin exactly where he had intended—on the side with the window. It was actually just a hole. Burlap kept the mosquitoes out in the summer, but in the winter, except for a make-shift rain gutter that had been tacked over the opening, there was nothing to impede Wan's view.

He heard the voices before he was close enough to see inside, but what he heard confused him. They were speaking loudly . . . but what were they saying? Was the rain distorting what he was able to hear? The deputy flattened his back onto the wall next to the cabin's window. *They are talking over the noise of the tin roof,* Wan realized. *Two men's voices?* Who was in the cabin? Wan mentally took roll. *Helen, Josef, the guy that took Helen . . . and some other guy?*

The deputy plainly identified two male voices. It was not that he couldn't *hear* them, he quickly figured. He could not *understand* them. They were speaking in another language . . . and one of them wasn't tinged with the British accent that had become so recognizable to him. As Wan eased to his right and peered into the opening, his heart sank as it all came together at once.

There were three people, as he had originally assumed. The other male voice he'd heard was his British friend. Friend? He didn't sound like the funny guy whom everyone in the area had gotten to know. In fact, he was speaking German. Wan recognized the dialect with its guttural sounds. *What the . . . ? Who?*

Wan did not understand whatever the two were saying to each other, but they did not appear to be chums. The one guy . . . he was holding a gun on Josef. Helen, he could see on Josef's left. He wished he could get her attention . . . or understand what they were saying . . . but, he determined, he'd sort it all out later. Now, the deputy knew, was the time to make his presence known and finish this business.

Wan had gotten the shotgun up to his shoulder and was about to yell out, "Freeze!" or "Hold it right there!" or any one of the phrases he had practiced in the mirror at home, when the conversation inside the cabin changed. To English. Wan listened with mounting horror as he put more pieces of the strange puzzle in place. Questions flooded his mind. One thing, however, was becoming abundantly clear: Whoever this man was, he was undeniably nuts. And he was about to kill Josef.

None of the three inside the cabin had any idea that Wan was watching the drama unfold from only ten feet away. The deputy ignored the rainwater cascading down his face and into his eyes while he tried to decide a course of action. The man with the gun was a Nazi. That was apparent. *If he ain't one, he's doing a great impression,* Wan noted grimly as the long-winded man, who was taunting Josef, continued to jabber away. *And what about Josef?* Wan thought again. *Who in the world is . . . ?* ". . . I will kill her first," the Nazi said. *What?!*

Without warning, the deputy's time of questioning was over, and his options were reduced to one. He saw the man turn the gun on Helen and was aware of Josef diving in front of her, but Wan had already fired.

In the split second one sometimes has to make a decision, Wan Cooper made one regarding his specific target that seemed strange to him in retrospect. He had been aware that the Nazi held his pistol in both hands. It occurred to the deputy that a body blast from his shotgun might cause the object of his ire to involuntarily squeeze the trigger of his pistol, shooting Helen in the process. So Wan shot his hands.

From ten feet away, twelve lead balls of double-aught shot have not yet spread into the wide pattern that makes that particular load so effective. In fact, at ten feet, the lethal spheres are arranged in a pattern that has widened to no more than five inches apart—about the size of a man's two hands clasped tightly into a fist.

While the deputy had never been especially proficient with a handgun, he had grown up hunting dove and quail in the fields and along the hedgerows of the south Alabama farms. Shooting a shotgun was all about instinct for Wan. When he shot a flying bird, he did so with both eyes open. Never bothering to squint and aim, the young deputy just pointed and fired. His accuracy, everyone said, was uncanny. He almost always hit what he shot at. And this time was no different.

It was a sight the deputy had never imagined but would never be able to forget. Schneider's hands simply disappeared. One second they were there . . . the next, they existed as red mist on the opposite wall.

After he saw that his target was down, the deputy ran around to the doorway and entered. Having fallen to the floor, Helen had risen to a sitting position. She seemed to be in shock and, though unhurt, did not say anything at first. Josef lay facedown, crying on the wooden floor, certain that Helen was dead. And the Nazi . . . well, Wan never forgot him.

The man was not dead when Wan entered the cabin. With the stumps that had been left at the end of his arms, he was pushing himself up into a sitting position. Wan approached cautiously, the shotgun carried loosely in his arms. The Nazi did not yell or scream or cry out. In fact, what he *did* do seemed bizarre . . . He bared his teeth.

Wan looked at him and blinked. Yes . . . the Nazi was baring his teeth. And there was a low growl coming from the man's throat. *Strange,* Wan thought. *Very strange. He is acting like a dog.* And so, the deputy shot him again.

Before doing so, he looked over to Helen, who was watching. Wan made a quick twirling motion with his finger that she correctly understood was his instruction for her to look away . . . turn her head. When she had, Wan reached the shotgun toward the dying man with one hand. Fleetingly it occurred to him how many times he had done the same for a dog or a deer that had been hit by a car on the highway. Wan put the tip of the gun barrel on the Nazi's chest and looked into his eyes. A caring person never hesitated to put a hurting animal out of its misery. Wan's daddy had taught him that. *I'm gonna put you out of mine,* Wan thought and pulled the trigger.

PART
THREE

Chapter 16

At a red light, I reached over into the passenger seat and flipped quickly through my calendar. It had been one day more than exactly five weeks, I saw, since I had uncovered the items under the wax myrtle behind my house.

The light turned green. I made a right turn onto Highway 59 and headed to Foley. The whole thing—the unearthed objects, the Internet searches, the conversations—was bothering me more than it should have. In effect, I had stopped trying to write at all, causing my editor and business manager to share in my consternation.

I simply could not concentrate. Not my greatest attribute under the best of circumstances, I now found myself staring at the computer screen only a few seconds before giving in to the Google button that beckoned me from the top of the page. Kriegsmarine, U-boats, Gulf of Mexico—I ran them again and again in every possible combination and read the same material until I knew it by heart.

Driving north, I looked at the businesses and billboards and tried to imagine what the area looked like back then. Would it have been possible, I wondered, for a submariner to come ashore and elude capture? Possible, I decided, but not likely. But what if it *could* have been done? I continued to ask myself. *How* might it have been accomplished? Only with help, I determined.

The week before, I had begun to feel as though there were something unseen just beyond my grasp—something maddening—as if there *were* an answer available, but first I had to articulate a question. Yet I didn't know what to ask. The feeling had crept up on me as I recalled a comment by one of the old people with whom I had spoken. We were finished with our conversation and were walking to the car when his remark had been thrown my way in passing.

At least, I *thought* it had been in passing. Now I was not so sure. In any event, I could no longer think of anything else. I was determined to find the truth. Or insult some very nice people.

"WELL, HELLO, ANDY! COME ON IN." SHE GLANCED AROUND me. "Is Polly with you?"

She doesn't even know I'm here, I wanted to say. *And she wouldn't have let me come if she had known I didn't call.* "No, ma'am," I answered. "Not today."

We walked straight on into the kitchen. "How was Louisiana?" I asked, which is how we, in the South, ask someone about a trip, as if we cared about the whole place.

"Oh, fine," she said. "We had a wonderful time. We stayed with the Wooleys—you know them—and saw all their people." Another Southern thing. We don't have families. We have people. She stopped, perhaps a bit confused about why I was there. "I'm sorry . . . were you here to see me? Or did you want—"

"Both of you. I apologize for dropping in like this . . ." *But I did it on purpose,* I wanted to add. I didn't.

"Oh, don't think a thing about it. Let me get him, though. He's in the backyard."

Soon she was back in the kitchen. "You want coffee or a Coke?"

"A Coke would be great," I answered. "Regular," I added, anticipating her next question. She nodded. She knew exactly what I meant.

In Alabama, we drink Coke. It's *all* Coke. In Chicago, they drink pop. In New Jersey, it's soda. But in Alabama, it is Coke.

"You want a Coke?" one person might ask.

"Sure," comes the response.

Second question: "What kind?"

Final answer: "Orange."

Translation: It's all Coke. This is how it's done here.

"Hey, Andy," he said, coming through the sliding glass door. "What's got you out and about?"

"You know," I said with a smile, "just doing some running around. Got my hair cut at Bozeman's, saw Dr. Surek . . . my throat thing still going on . . . and . . . what else . . . oh, I stopped at Patty Cakes Bakery for Polly. Anyway, I was in the area and just wanted to say hello."

We all sat down at the table, talked about their trip to Louisiana for a while, our boys, the church, the possibility of an undefeated season for the Crimson Tide . . . Were they nervous? I couldn't tell.

Then I said, "Hey, I have something I want you to see." Holding hands, both were sitting across from me. I removed a manila envelope from the leather writing tablet I always carry and opened it. Slowly, one at a time, I removed the silver buttons I had found under the wax myrtle from the envelope and slowly, one at a time, placed them in a line across the table.

Without speaking, I took the ring out next. I placed it in front of the buttons, careful to set it upright, straight, and symmetrically in the display I was creating. Next, the

Iron Cross was situated beside the ring and the *UB* badge next to it.

I must admit that my hands were shaking as I forced myself to move even slower. Neither the old man nor his wife looked at me. They were still holding hands . . . watching mine . . . and made not a sound.

I put the picture of Hitler and the officers inspecting the sailors above the buttons and the photograph of the Kriegsmarine cadet in front of her. Then I brought out the small photograph—the one of the man, the woman, and the baby in the wagon. For a moment, I held it and watched the old man and old woman in front of me.

They were frozen, barely breathing.

Did I really want to do what I was about to do? Was this right? Would it serve a purpose beyond the satisfaction of my own curiosity?

As gently as I could, I laid the tiny family portrait in front of him and quietly sat back in my chair. For a moment, nothing happened. Both of them were seemingly deep in thought, but calm . . . motionless. Then the old woman haltingly reached across and picked up the family picture with her right hand. She had been holding her husband's hand with her left, but let go and put that arm around his shoulders.

At that moment, as close as they were to me physically—emotionally, they were miles away. I can only describe what they did for the next several minutes as a huddle . . . she with her left arm around him and continuing to nestle the family portrait in the palm of her right hand. Holding it close, they whispered to each other—the old woman doing most of the talking—and pointed to several details in the picture. I do not know what they said to each other during this time, for I did not try to hear.

When they were finished and looked up, both had tears in their eyes. "Mrs. Newman?" I said softly. "When did you bury these things on the island?"

She took a deep breath. Her lip quivered, but when she spoke, her voice was strong. "I did it one night before the war was over. Folks were getting real worked up about people from other countries . . . they were suspecting everybody and his brother as a spy. Newman spoke with an English accent back then, and, well . . . I didn't want to take the chance. Some had already had their homes gone through by the authorities, their yards dug up by suspicious locals. I didn't want to just throw the things in the Gulf . . ." She glanced at her husband. ". . . though *he* said to."

She shrugged. "We were hoping to have children one day. I wanted them to have something of their father's . . ." She looked at the things on the table. "Right there . . . that's everything he had. I canned it all up . . . even this picture." She held up the one of the family and frowned. "Seems crazy now to have buried this one. I mean, what could it have hurt to keep *this* one? But we were so scared. You can't imagine . . ." I nodded. She was wrong. In fact, I could *only* imagine.

"Anyway, I rowed over one night to that little island you live on now. It was trash land then. They grazed cattle on it. We never thought in a million years anyone would ever live there. As time went on, we tried occasionally to find the spot I had chosen that night, but, you know, storms and all . . . we just never found it."

"Until now," I said.

"Until now," she agreed. "How did you know?"

I paused, trying to get my thoughts in order. I had a thousand questions I wanted to ask, but I knew it was important to *answer* this one. Indicating Mr. Newman, who had not raised his head, I said to her, "He told me."

Still he did not move. But she did. Her mouth dropped open; her eyes were wide. She was as flustered as anyone I've ever seen. "What? I don't . . . What?" She looked back and forth between her husband, who *still* wasn't moving, and me, sputtering, "I just don't understand . . ."

"Mr. Newman?"

He looked up. "Call me Josef," he said.

"All right." Then, looking back to Mrs. Newman, I gave her the answer both needed to hear. "Mr. Newman . . . Josef . . . walked me to my car the last time we got together . . . right before you went to Louisiana. Before I got in, he said, 'Those things all held up pretty good, didn't they? After all those many years sealed in a vegetable can?'"

Mrs. Newman was confused. "But I don't—"

"I never told anyone—anyone—that the things were buried in a can. I only said that they were buried." I looked over at Josef, slightly stooped now with snow-white hair. "I have an idea that you knew that."

She turned to him. "Honey, why did you . . . ?" She turned back to me. "I mean, it's all right . . . I just want to know why he—"

"Helen," he interrupted gently, "I'm an old man. Danny's gone. We're alone. I'm not ashamed of the life we've built—"

"Oh, sweetheart," she said quickly, "I never meant to say—"

"Hush," he said, covering her hands with his own. "Listen to me now . . ." He stopped abruptly, remembering I was there and smiled at me. "I'm sorry to be doing this in front of you . . ."

I held up my hands. "No," I said. "I don't mean to be in the way. Do you want me to leave? We can talk later . . ."

"No," Josef said. "Stay. We're fine." Mrs. Newman nodded, then focused her attention on the man she had loved for more than fifty years. He said, "Helen Newman, you are the wisest woman I know. You are as beautiful now as the night you beat the daylights out of me on the beach. You have taken some unforgivable beginnings, some unforgivable situations, some unforgivable people . . . and forgiven them all.

"Together, we have struggled and learned to live life as it should be lived . . . except for one thing . . . one secret we have hidden for more than half a century. I am tired of hiding. You are, too, woman," he said with a grin. "Night before we left, I heard you on the phone"—he motioned toward me—"telling him about a spy that got shot in the woods near Fort Morgan." He noted his wife's embarrassed expression with a laugh and turned to me. "By the way, that's a story you need to hear."

Back to Helen, he said, "Don't you think people will forgive us? I'm not saying we make an announcement, but I think a few people . . ." He looked at me. "Helen, I want this young man to ask some questions. I want him to find out what you know. There're a lot of people who need to take an unhappy life and turn it into a great one, like you've done."

I spoke up. "I already know what my first two questions are . . ."

"All right," Josef said.

I took that as my cue. "Number one, who is Danny? Number two . . . did she really beat the daylights out of you on the beach? I want to hear *that* story!"

They laughed, but Helen immediately got up and returned a moment later with a framed photograph. "This is Danny Gilbert," she said. "He was our son. He had Down syndrome."

I took the picture and saw that the subject was a grown man. His affliction was evident, but the light in his eyes was undeniable. "He was your son?" I asked.

They smiled. "He was," Josef said. "Danny was actually the biological son of some very dear friends of ours, Billy and Margaret Gilbert. They owned a café down what is now Highway 59. When Margaret passed away in 1954, Billy was lost. He missed her terribly, of course, but was really concerned about Danny. Billy was getting up in years, and we all knew Danny couldn't live by himself . . . so Danny came to live with us. We never had any other children, and he called her 'Mama Helen,' so we called him our son. He seemed to like it."

"So did we," Helen said.

"So did we," Josef agreed. Pointing into the den toward the back of the house, he said, "All those things are Danny's in there. Danny did those."

Leading me into the den, Helen turned on the overhead lights and stepped back. I was in awe. The entire room was filled with carvings. And they were stunning. Mostly birds and animals, here and there a flower, there was even a bust of Abraham Lincoln.

"You have got to be kidding," I gasped. "These are . . . they are incredible. I've never seen anything like this. How many are there?"

"We have about six hundred left," Helen said proudly. "There's a store in New Orleans that we allow to sell two pieces a month. They haven't gotten less than fifteen hundred dollars for one in more than three years now. The money goes to education for children like Danny."

"Hey, look at this," Josef said, digging in his pocket. "This is my favorite. It's the first thing he ever did. I wouldn't take a million dollars for it—not even for charity."

I took the small item from the old man and recognized it immediately as a speckled trout. The piece was small. Worn and nicked from the years spent in Josef's pocket, it did not possess the sophistication of the artist's later work, but because it was the very first "Danny Gilbert" and treasured by the owner, its value was indeed priceless.

I didn't want to make the old couple sad, but I was curious. "When did Danny . . . ahhh—"

"Danny died in 1961," Helen said, smiling. "He was forty-nine."

We talked for hours . . . through lunch, which we ate on the back porch, and on into the afternoon. It seemed I actually did have a thousand questions. "Is your name really Newman?"

"No," he said. "The fishermen at the docks all called me the 'new man' for a long while. Then it was 'Josef *the* new man' and finally just 'Josef Newman.' When Helen and I got married, I put 'Josef Newman' on the certificate, and no one ever questioned it."

"So you *are* really married?" I asked.

"Oh, yes," Helen replied, "but not until 1947. It was well after the war before we felt safe enough to try to get the paperwork."

"Wan made that happen," Josef said.

"Wan was your best man, sweetheart."

"That's true. That's true."

As the afternoon wore on, I found myself attempting to keep all the stories straight. The conversation was moving in ten different directions at once. I thought then, and still do, that it might have been the first time Josef and Helen talked about some of this. "Wait," I said. They looked at me patiently. "You mean Wan . . . the same guy who shot at you with the pistol?"

"Yes." They laughed.

"What about the English accent?"

"What about it?" Josef asked.

"What happened to it? That's such a great part of the story."

Josef grinned. "I kept it up for years." He shrugged. "But it faded away. Along with all the people who remembered it, I suppose."

I asked permission to change the subject and started down another path. "Can I ask what you did with Schneider's body?" Josef grimaced, and Helen looked very uncomfortable. I backed up. "That's okay, I just—"

"No," Josef broke in, "You're fine, it's just . . . you know . . . not really anything I ever thought I'd be talking about."

"I understand."

He looked at his wife. "You okay?" She nodded, and he turned back to me. "We just dragged him off and buried him. I mean, we got out a ways from my little cabin." I must have been frowning. Josef continued to explain, "You got to understand. That was a different time. No forensics, a deputy in on it . . ."

"In on it?" Helen said. "Wan shot him."

Josef nodded toward her. "You know what I mean. Like I said, it was a different time. Anyway, I still feel like Wan did the right thing."

"I do too," Helen was quick to add. "I didn't mean to intimate that he didn't."

"And it wasn't like anyone was looking for Ernst Schneider." Josef shook his head as if to rid himself of a nasty memory. "He was a bad one."

"And nobody ever found out?" Neither spoke. I asked again: "So you don't think anybody ever knew?"

Helen couldn't stand it. She answered, "I think Billy knew. I think Wan told him."

I looked at Josef, who nodded in agreement. "Yeah," he said, "I think so too. I think Wan felt like he *had* to tell him."

"How so?" I asked.

"After we buried Schneider—that very day—Wan went and arrested Harris Kramer. He found the radio Schneider had been using up in Kramer's attic and pinned it on Kramer. He'd been trying to get Kramer for a long time anyway. And he *was* guilty . . . Wan just got him for something else."

I shook my head in amazement.

"Anyway, when Wan took old Kramer in, Billy put two and two together—connecting one German spy with another—and was about to make a big stink about it—you know, get the posse, let's go find this other one—but nobody else knew there *was* another one . . . much less that he was already dead. So Wan told Billy what happened in order to keep him quiet." He paused, then added, "Kramer yelled bloody murder about another Nazi ashore, but everybody figured he was trying to save his own skin. Nobody believed him."

"And Wan never said anything about you?" I asked.

He shook his head. "Nope, never did. Probably as much out of respect for Helen as anything. He'd heard me through the window that day, telling Schneider that I loved her . . . I don't know. Maybe that was it. He didn't take his eye off me for a long time, though. He loved Helen too."

"Oh, Josef . . . ," Helen scoffed.

"It's true. You know it."

"Well, I'm just glad Shirley came along for Wan."

"Who's Shirley?" I asked. My mind was swimming.

"Shirley was a local girl," Helen said. "From Robertsdale anyway. She and Wan were married before we were. Nineteen forty-six, I think."

"Sounds right," Josef agreed.

"Is Wan still alive?" I asked.

"No," Josef said. "Wan got cancer. Passed away about fifteen years ago."

"Shirley's still alive, though. She's not a Cooper anymore." Helen smiled mischievously. "She's a Warren now." She waited for what she'd just said to sink in.

It did. "Oh, come on!" I exclaimed, as Josef chuckled. "Seriously?" I said. "Shirley Warren that works at the state park? *That* Shirley Warren?"

"That's the one." Helen grinned.

I couldn't stand it. I had to ask, "Does she know that you—"

"Nooo. Nooo," they said. "Wan never told her."

I was curious about Josef's friends and family left in Germany. "Did they ever know you made it off the sub?"

He shrugged. "No family left. And as for friends, there was Hans Kuhlmann, of course, but everyone else in Germany was so displaced by the fighting that when it was all over, people just assumed that the friends they no longer saw—were dead."

"What about Kuhlmann . . . your sub commander? Did you ever see him again? Or communicate to him in some way that you were safe . . . alive?"

Josef spoke softly to Helen, then turned to me. As he continued to talk, she slipped from the table and out of the room. "I never saw Hans again. Neither did I hear anything about him for years."

Helen walked back into the room and handed me a copied article from a newspaper. It was an Associated Press article, carried by the *Birmingham News,* dated June 9, 2001. The headline read: "Remains of Sunken WWII German Sub Found in Gulf." I glanced at Josef, who remarked, "Hans never made it home."

Reading just the first two paragraphs gave me chills:

> *New Orleans. A sunken World War II submarine has been discovered 5,000 feet deep in the Gulf of Mexico, rerouting a planned oil company pipeline and rewriting a bit of wartime history.*
>
> *BP and Shell Oil Company, which had been surveying the Gulf floor for a joint pipeline project, announced the discovery Friday of the U-166, which was sunk in 1942 after it sank an American ship.*

"She was sunk by depth charges dropped from a navy patrol boat," Josef said. "The U-166 attacked and sank the *Robert E. Lee,* then was *herself* attacked and destroyed from above."

"Tell him about Gertrude," Helen prompted.

"Gertrude?"

"Gertrude was Hans's wife," Josef said. "Beautiful girl. I was in their wedding. I talked to her as recently as last year."

"She's still alive?" I asked incredulously.

"She was last year," Josef said. "After the sub was found, I made an effort to find her, and did. She is still in Cologne . . . invests quite heavily in the stock market. All blue chip American companies, she says." He laughed as I shook my head in wonder.

IT WAS DARK WHEN I FINALLY LEFT WITH A PROMISE TO RETURN. I was exhausted, my mind still reeling from what I had discovered in the lives of these two extraordinary people. That day was a conclusion of sorts—the unveiling of a mystery whose answers for so long had remained just out of reach. But it was also a beginning. And I am encouraged by what I feel when I contemplate the difference their decisions—and very lives—have made.

Josef had already said good-bye when Helen walked me to the door. She hugged me and told me how much she had enjoyed the day. "It is a bit strange to talk about that time," she said thoughtfully, ". . . after all these years."

I stopped on the front porch. Now that Josef wasn't around, there was something else on her mind . . . I could feel it. "Are you all right?"

"I'm fine. Just . . . tired, I suppose." I waited. "Andy?"

"Yes, ma'am?"

"Are you planning to write about this? Our lives, I mean?"

So *that* was it. "Well," I answered carefully, "I won't if you don't want me to."

She thought a moment. "Do you think our story could

help? By that, I mean, could we help folks somehow?"

"Mrs. Newman," I said earnestly, "I believe that there are people who struggle every day with the challenges you and Josef have conquered. And frankly I am one of them. Yes, I think your story will help. Who benefits when we come to understand and harness the power of forgiveness? Children, marriages, careers, nations . . . the list goes on and on."

"I don't want Josef to be hurt. He's lived in America for so long now. What if there are those who don't understand?" Then she brightened. "I have an idea . . . if you write about this, can you change the names?"

"Sure." I nodded. "That won't be any problem."

Helen sighed. "I'm sorry," she said. "I don't mean to act scared. I'm an old woman now, and I just get like this sometimes." She hugged me again and wiped what I hoped was a happy tear from her cheek.

"Listen," I said in farewell. "I promise, you will not have cause to be fearful or embarrassed by anything I write. And besides," I added, "I will make sure the publisher classifies the book as 'Self-Help' or 'Personal Growth' or one of the other 'Fiction' categories. No one will ever believe a word of it.

WHERE ARE THEY NOW?

Hans Gunther Kuhlmann

His body still rests with the remains of his crew (minus Josef Bartels Landermann) in five thousand feet of water due south from the Louisiana coastline. Considered a "war grave" and protected by international treaty, the U-166 will not be recovered or disturbed. Its location was discovered June 6, 2001, in a joint venture between BP and Shell Oil as they were surveying the gulf floor for a pipeline project.

Ironically, the U-166 was found less than a mile from the wreck of the *Robert E. Lee,* the last vessel attacked and destroyed by Kuhlmann and his crew. A sixteen-foot sweep (steering) oar from one of *Robert E. Lee*'s lifeboats is mounted on a wall in the living room of author Andy Andrews.

As of this writing, Kuhlmann's wife, Gertrude, is still alive. She is remarried and lives quietly under her new name in Cologne, Germany.

Wan Cooper

Sherriff's Deputy Wan Cooper remained close friends with Josef and Helen until his death from lung cancer in 1989. His widow, Shirley, remarried and has recently been widowed again. She is retired from her long-time job at the Gulf State Park in Gulf Shores, Alabama, and now volunteers with the "Mother's Day Out" program at a local church.

Margaret and Billy Gilbert

They had closed the café and retired when Margaret passed away suddenly in 1954. Recovering from a broken hip she had suffered in a fall, doctors surmised it was a blood clot that stopped her heart. For a time, Danny Gilbert seemed to relish the role of comforter for his father, but Billy—brokenhearted and in poor health already—soon thereafter succumbed to the ravages of emphysema. He died in 1955. Billy and Margaret are buried next to each other in a Baldwin County cemetery.

Danny Gilbert

Billy Gilbert signed legal custody of Danny over to Josef and Helen six months before he died. Danny had already moved in with the Newman's—a decision that had been made in order to lessen the trauma of Billy's death to Danny.

Danny lived happily for several more years, finally dying in his sleep at forty-nine, long past the age any doctor had ever predicted. He was buried in the same cemetery plot with Billy and Margaret. Danny's intricate carvings are now scattered all over the southeastern United States, most in homes of people who have no knowledge of the artist or history of the pieces in their possession. Interestingly, Danny never carved his name into a single creation, always insisting, "God made this, not me." The small speckled trout— the Christmas gift from Danny to Josef—now rests proudly on a shelf in Andy Andrews's office.

Harris Kramer

Kramer was captured within hours of Schneider's death. Both Helen and Josef had seen the old boat captain in Foley with Schneider, and when they described him to Wan, the deputy knew exactly who he was looking for. When Wan found Schneider's radio in Kramer's attic, it was all the evidence he needed for an arrest.

Curiously, Kramer never made it to trial. He was held in Bay Minette, Alabama, in the Baldwin County Jail. Placed in a cell with seven other men, within a week he was dead. Found swinging from the bars with a bed sheet around his neck, it was officially ruled a suicide, though no one ever adequately explained how he managed to hang himself with his hands tied behind his back.

He was buried in an unmarked grave with no coffin and—so the story goes—placed in the ground face down. Even after death, it seemed, no one liked Harris Kramer.

Ernst Schneider

Schneider's body was dragged from the cabin where he was killed and buried in as deep a grave as Wan and Josef could dig in the sand with their hands. According to the locals, there were no coyotes in those woods at that time (there are now), and as long as someone's dog didn't find the grave quickly, Schneider's bones are very likely still there.

From Highway 59 in Gulf Shores, Alabama, turn west onto highway 180 (the Fort Morgan Road). After almost six miles, you will come to the Bon Secour National Wildlife Refuge on your left. This seven-thousand-acre tract of land was established by Congress in 1980 to be left untouched. It remains a perfect example of what it all looked like when Helen's cabin and a few others were spread through the area.

Keep driving. At the nine-mile mark, you will see a small dirt parking area. Stop here, get out, and walk the Pine Beach Trail. You can walk all the way to the gulf. Watch carefully because this is the area in which I am told the Nazi was buried. Depending on recent rain or wind, you just might be the first to spot Schneider's bones peeking through the sand.

Helen and Josef Newman

Josef Bartels Landermann is still listed as an official casualty of the U-166. He was never reported missing from the sub and so, when it was sunk on the evening of July 30, 1942, Landermann went on the casualty list and has remained there ever since. See for yourself—read the entire crew list and look at pictures of Kuhlman and the sub at *http://www.pastfoundation.org/U166/CrewList.htm.*

Schneider, the political officer onboard, was never listed as a crew member. Therefore, due to the purposeful destruction of documents during the last days of the Third Reich, it is not clear whether or not Nazi files ever recorded Schneider as missing or killed in action. In any case, it is safe to say that Josef Bartels Landermann is the only "official" discrepancy of the U-166.

Josef Newman is still healthy, happy, and somewhat amused by this whole uncovering of his earlier life. Helen is somewhat less comfortable with the idea that anyone knows the truth. Soon after I presented Josef and Helen with a first draft of the manuscript, they made plans to move and have since done so. Insisting they planned this move all along, they are happy living in Louisiana and have requested that I say no more than that.

READER'S GUIDE

The following discussion guide was designed to help you integrate the lessons found in *The Heart Mender* and to facilitate group discussion. Please use them merely as a guide. Stay open to where your thoughts and a live discussion might take you. The questions are divided into specific topics of interest, so feel free to start wherever you like.

On Symbolic Imagery

1. Consider the symbolic use of names in this story, particularly Helen and Josef. The Greek name *Helen* means "torchlight," or "bright one." Just like Helen Mason in *The Heart Mender*, Helen of Troy, who was also known for her physical beauty, was loved by more than one man. Think also of Helen Keller, a woman both blind and deaf, as was our story's Helen (though only figuratively).

   The Greek meaning of Joseph is "God will increase." In the Old Testament, though sold into slavery by his brothers, Joseph later triumphed over this adversity. In the New Testament, another Joseph became an icon of mercy by standing by a woman when he need not have.

   What other significances do you find in Josef's and Helen's names? What other interesting uses of names are found in this story?

2. Authors often use irony to help readers understand the message they are trying to convey as characters "learn the lesson." What ironies can you see in *The Heart Mender*? How are they effective or not effective?

3. Literature is full of tales that begin as something or someone washes ashore—literally a gift (or a curse) from the sea. As a literary symbol, the sea often signifies life. A sea journey might symbolize the journey from birth to death or vice versa. Discuss the role the sea (and the shore) plays in this story.

4. What archetypal, or symbolic, role does Danny play in the narrative? How does Danny touch—and change— almost every character, from his parents to Ernst Schneider? How does his innocence impact each person?

5. What other lessons can we all learn from Danny? Does he have something to teach us? Could it be that the qualities of a Down syndrome person—persistence, for example, or lack of fear of failure (see page 118)—are qualities that we might want to emulate?

On the Nature of Decisions

6. The story's plot hinges on decisions made by characters at pivotal times: Helen chooses not to turn Josef in, for example. What other meaningful decisions in *The Heart Mender* can you recall? What do you think was the source of Helen's initial hesitation, given the highly emotional state she was in?

7. Although Josef had contemplated suicide, when he found himself overboard, he chose to struggle to stay alive, even though he was wounded. Why?

8. Someone once said, "All that is necessary for the triumph of evil is that good men do nothing." The author

identifies several "good men" in this story; at times when each could have chosen to do nothing, what might have happened?

On the Notion That "No Man Is an Island"

9. *The Heart Mender* takes place on an island, but the significance of an island refers to more than just a physical location. On page 156, the author refers to the John Donne quote "No man is an island." Where is the actual island on which the story takes place? How would you describe this setting as a symbolic location?

10. The John Donne quotation was written in 1623, when philosophers were beginning to note the interconnectedness of mankind, that is, that people are not isolated from one another but instead affect the lives of others in ways seen and unseen. Donne wrote:

    "No man is an island, entire of itself; every man is a piece of the continent, a part of the main. If a clod be washed away by the sea, Europe is the less . . . Any man's death diminishes me, because I am involved in mankind; and therefore never send to know for whom the bell tolls; it tolls for thee" (*Meditation XVII*).

    By setting the story on an island, the author seems to want us to think of the power of *individuals*—to affect a situation, history, themselves, or others—yet the poem itself is about the power of *community*. What do you think is the true meaning of this paradoxical message?

On Democracy, War, and the Course of Civilization

11. Discuss the distinction the author makes between Germans and Nazis (pages 15 and 31). Is this something

you've considered before, with regards to World War II Germany? The author wants us to understand that the world isn't drawn in black and white but has shades of meaning that can be interpreted differently by each person who views it. On page 43, the German submarine commander says, "War is one thing. Murder is quite another." How can this realization change the way we interpret current events?

12. Josef had this to say about the nature of democracy and civilization: "These nations progressed through the following sequence: from bondage to spiritual faith; from spiritual faith to great courage; from great courage to liberty; from liberty to abundance; from abundance to complacency; from complacency to apathy; from apathy to dependence; and finally from dependence back into bondage" (page 141–42). Do you think there are parallels to be drawn (as Josef insists) to our own democracy? Where do you think the United States is on this timeline?

On the Power of Forgiveness

13. Andy Andrews strongly believes that true forgiveness mends hearts and gives people second chances. Do you agree? Can you think of other equally dynamic principles that have the power to change lives so dramatically?

14. The power of love is one alternate principle presented in the story: both Helen and Josef are willing to sacrifice their own lives to save the other. Can you think of other loving sacrifices depicted in the story?

15. How can you apply the power of love and forgiveness to your life right now? Think about it both internally, in your family and social circles, and in world affairs and politics at large.

16. Several characters in this story learned of the redemptive and healing power of true forgiveness. Discuss the principle of forgiveness—how it's not necessary that the object of forgiveness *ask* for it, *deserve* it, or even be *aware* that he's been forgiven. Discuss a time when you gave or received this kind of forgiveness.

Log on to AndyAndrews.com to find
new tools and resources for
discovering a more compelling future.

ABOUT THE AUTHOR

❧

Hailed by a *New York Times* reporter as "someone who has become one of the most influential people in America," ANDY ANDREWS is a best-selling novelist and in-demand corporate speaker for the world's largest organizations. He has spoken at the request of four different U.S. presidents and at military bases worldwide. Andy is the author of the *New York Times* bestsellers *The Travelers Gift* and *The Noticer*, as well as *The Lost Choice* and *Return to Sawyerton Springs*. He lives in Orange Beach, Alabama, with his wife, Polly, and their two sons.

Andy can be contacted
or engaged for an event at
AndyAndrews.com

ACKNOWLEDGMENTS

IN AN UNDERTAKING OF THIS SORT, THE LIST OF PEOPLE to whom gratitude is owed can be overwhelming. I am blessed to be surrounded by friends and family who have become a team of which I am thrilled to be a part. If one perceives me as a person who makes good and informed choices, it is only because of the reliance on the counsel of these people. Thank you all for your presence in my life:

. . . To Polly, my wife and best friend,

. . . to THE Robert D. Smith, my personal manager and champion,

. . . to Gail and Mike Hyatt, who gave life to my career as an author,

. . . to Matt Baugher, Chief of Making It Happen!

. . . to Brian Hampton, my original editor, whose careful eye and quick mind made this a much better book,

. . . to David Moberg, Dale Wilstermann, Emily Sweeney, Stephanie Newton, Jennifer McNeil, and Kristi Johnson, who brilliantly oversee the publishing of my books,

. . . to Rick Spruill, Julie Jayne, Doug Miller, Tom Knight, Jeff Miller, and the rest of the Thomas Nelson sales team, who work so hard to get my books out to the masses,

. . . to Todd Rainsberger, who helped shape the narrative,

. . . to Sandi Dorff, Paula Tebbe, and Susie White, who direct the daily parts of my life,

. . . to Jared McDaniel for his beyond brilliant eye for graphic detail and the ability to continuously create a WOW factor visually,

. . . to Nate Bailey, Matt Lempert, Paul Fries, and Chad Laboy, who meticulously oversee the details of the office and my business life,

. . . to Kurt V. Besley and Brent C. Gray, who handle the legal rights to all my intellectual property,

. . . to Paul Krupin and George Uribe, who push hard in very creative ways to get the word out to and through the media,

. . . and to Mrs. Edna McLoyd, my eighth grade English teacher from Dothan, Alabama, who told me I could write.

. . . Thanks also to Scott Jeffrey for his coaching and personal attention to detail,

. . . to Zachary Smith and Nicholas Francis for their Web mastery,

. . . and to Katrina and Jerry Anderson, Vicki and Brian Bakken, Erik Born, Don Brindley, Sunny Brownlee, Foncie and Joe Bullard, Brent Burns, Myrth and Cliff Callaway, Julie and Doug Cassens, Lillian and Edward Gilley, Gloria and Martin Gonzalez, Lynn and Mike Jakubik, Patsy Jones, Nancy Lopez, Karen and Alan McBride, Liz and Bob McEwen, Melanie and Mike Martin, Mary and Jim Pace, Glenda and Kevin Perkins, Brenda and Todd Rainsberger, Kathy and Dick Rollins, Barbara Selvey, Claudia and Pat Simpson, Shannon and John Smith, Christopher Surek, Maryann and Jerry Tyler, Mary Ann and Dave Winck, Kristi and Steve Woods, Kathy and Mike Wooley. Your example and influence in my life are undeniable and very much appreciated.

Very special thanks to those whose memories and information were crucial to this story—who, because of the lives they now lead, have elected to remain anonymous.

REFERENCES

HAVING RESEARCHED THE TOPIC OF FORGIVENESS FOR MANY years, my thoughts and, indeed, the contents of this book have been molded by the works of many people much wiser than I.

Their writing and spoken words have been life-changing for many, and in order to give them proper credit and the reader an opportunity to delve further into their work, the names of these people, in alphabetical order, are presented below. Their lives and influence are greatly appreciated.

Paul Boese	John Mason
Foncie Bullard	Malachy McCourt
Joe Bullard	Mark Muesse
Barbara Crafton	John Musser
Edward Gibbon	Sara Paddison
Bill Gothard	Harper Shannon
Drew J. Gunnells	Lewis B. Smedes
George Herbert	Robert D. Smith
Scott Jeffrey	Andy Stanley
Clare Boothe Luce	Paula Tebbe
Carol Luebering	Randy Thomas
Frederic Luskin	Rick Warren

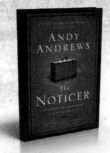
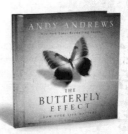

Also by
ANDY ANDREWS

THE TRAVELER'S GIFT

This unique narrative is a blend of entertaining fiction, allegory, and inspiration. Master storyteller Andy Andrews gives us a front row seat for one man's journey of a lifetime. David Ponder has lost his job and with it, the will to live. Then something incredible happens. He is supernaturally selected to travel through time and gets the amazing opportunity to visit some of history's most remarkable people. There's Abraham Lincoln, King Solomon, and Anne Frank, among others. Each visit yields a distinct Decision for Success that will one day impact the entire world. On this journey, David Ponder is changed forever. You will be too.

ISBN: 0-7852-6428-0

THE LOST CHOICE

In *The Lost Choice*, *New York Times* bestselling author Andy Andrews brilliantly weaves a suspenseful tale of intrigue, inspiration, and enlightenment to offer readers a stunning glimpse into the power of their own actions. He provides clear, guiding principles for rediscovering our own "lost choices," and proves that everything we do—and don't do—affects not only our own lives, but also the lives of generations to come. In this unforgettable work, Andrews offers an inspiring, suspenseful tale of empowerment, connection, consequence, and purpose.

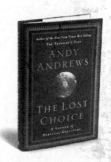

ISBN: 0-7852-6139-7

SOCKS FOR CHRISTMAS

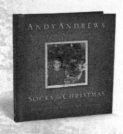

For ten-year old Andy, Christmas was about fun, food, and who gets bragging rights to the most loot under the tree. As for that boring old gift of socks, he might have to say thank you, but he didn't have to like them.

But something would happen one Christmas that would change Andy forever. Yes, Christmas in 1968 was an awakening for Andy Andrews. But more than that, it was the Christmas he learned a truly significant secret: how to have a grateful heart . . . even for a simple pair of socks.

ISBN: 1-4016-0239-8